P9-AEY-880

THE CREATION OF THE U.S. CONSTITUTION

THE CREATION
OF THE U.S.
CONSTITUTION

Other books in the
Opposing Viewpoints in World History series:

OPPOSING VIEWPOINTS®
IN WORLD HISTORY

THE CREATION OF THE U.S. CONSTITUTION

Don Nardo, *Book Editor*

Bruce Glassman, *Vice President*
Bonnie Szumski, *Publisher*
Helen Cothran, *Managing Editor*

GREENHAVEN PRESS
An imprint of Thomson Gale, a part of The Thomson Corporation

Detroit • New York • San Francisco • San Diego • New Haven, Conn.
Waterville, Maine • London • Munich

LIBRARY OF CONGRESS CATALOGING-IN-PUBLICATION DATA

The creation of the U.S. Constitution / Don Nardo, book editor.
   p. cm. — (Opposing viewpoints in world history)
   Includes bibliographical references and index.
   ISBN 0-7377-2579-6 (lib. : alk. paper) — ISBN 0-7377-2580-X (pbk. : alk. paper)
    1. Constitutional history—United States. I. Nardo, Don, 1947– . II. Opposing viewpoints in world history series.
   KF4541.C683 2005
   342.7302'9—dc22
                                     2004047422

✲ Contents

Chapter 2: What Provisions Should the Constitution Have?

✵ Foreword

On December 2, 1859, several hundred soldiers gathered at the outskirts of Charles Town, Virginia, to carry out, and provide security for, the execution of a shabbily dressed old man with a beard that hung to his chest. The execution of John Brown quickly became and has remained one of those pivotal historical events that are immersed in controversy. Some of Brown's contemporaries claimed that he was a religious fanatic who deserved to be executed for murder. Others claimed Brown was a heroic and selfless martyr whose execution was a tragedy. Historians have continued to debate which picture of Brown is closest to the truth.

The wildly diverging opinions on Brown arise from fundamental disputes involving slavery and race. In 1859 the United States was becoming increasingly polarized over the issue of slavery. Brown believed in both the necessity of violence to end slavery and in the full political and social equality of the races. This made him part of the radical fringe even in the North. Brown's conviction and execution stemmed from his role in leading twenty-one white and black followers to attack and occupy a federal weapons arsenal in Harpers Ferry, Virginia. Brown had hoped to ignite a large slave uprising. However, the raid begun on October 16, 1859, failed to draw support from local slaves; after less than thirty-six hours, Brown's forces were overrun by federal and local troops. Brown was wounded and captured, and ten of his followers were killed.

Brown's raid—and its intent to arm slaves and foment insurrection—was shocking to the South and much of the North. An editorial in the *Patriot*, an Albany, Georgia, newspaper, stated that Brown was a "notorious old thief and murderer" who deserved to be hanged. Many southerners expressed fears that Brown's actions were part of a broader northern conspiracy against the South—fears that seemed to be confirmed by captured letters documenting Brown's ties with some prominent northern abolitionists, some of whom had provided him with financial support. Such alarms also found confirmation in the pronouncements of some speakers such as writer Henry David Thoreau, who asserted that

11

Brown had "a perfect right to interfere by force with the slaveholder, in order to rescue the slave." But not all in the North defended Brown's actions. Abraham Lincoln and William Seward, leading politicians of the nascent Republican Party, both denounced Brown's raid. Abolitionists, including William Lloyd Garrison, called Brown's adventure "misguided, wild, and apparently insane." They were afraid Brown had done serious damage to the abolitionist cause.

Today, though all agree that Brown's ideas on racial equality are no longer radical, historical opinion remains divided on just what Brown thought he could accomplish with his raid, or even whether he was fully sane. Historian Russell Banks argues that even today opinions of Brown tend to split along racial lines. African Americans tend to view him as a hero, Banks argues, while whites are more likely to judge him mad. "And it's for the same reason—because he was a white man who was willing to sacrifice his life to liberate Black Americans. The very thing that makes him seem mad to white Americans is what makes him seem heroic to Black Americans."

The controversy over John Brown's life and death remind readers that history is replete with debate and controversy. Not only have major historical developments frequently been marked by fierce debates as they happened, but historians examining the same events in retrospect have often come to opposite conclusions about their causes, effects, and significance. By featuring both contemporaneous and retrospective disputes over historical events in a pro/con format, the Opposing Viewpoints in World History series can help readers gain a deeper understanding of important historical issues, see how historical judgments unfold, and develop critical thinking skills. Each article is preceded by a concise summary of its main ideas and information about the author. An in-depth book introduction and prefaces to each chapter provide background and context. An annotated table of contents and index help readers quickly locate material of interest. Each book also features an extensive bibliography for further research, questions designed to spark discussion and promote close reading and critical thinking, and a chronology of events.

Introduction

Creating the Constitution: A Process Fraught with Disagreement

Today most Americans think of the U.S. Constitution as an ironclad, almost iconic blueprint for fair and balanced government. Many of the provisions in the document provide for basic democratic principles, such as election of the chief executive and members of Congress, checks and balances among the branches of government, freedom of speech, freedom of the press, freedom of religion, and so forth. One might wonder who would argue over or deny the importance of what seem to be fundamental truths of an open, just society and government. To the citizens of modern democracies like the United States and Britain it might appear that, as Thomas Jefferson put it in the Declaration of Independence, these concepts are "self-evident."

It comes as a bit of surprise to some, therefore, to discover that the making of the U.S. Constitution was fraught with disagreement, debate, and controversy, sometimes of a heated nature. Some of the nation's founding fathers (who were also the Constitution's framers) did not think the country even needed the Constitution. A less-structured and less-sweeping constitution—the Articles of Confederation—was adopted in the 1770s. And a number of early congressmen felt that this document, with some tweaking and fine-tuning, was sufficient. Even those who held that a tougher, more comprehensive constitution was needed rarely agreed on what form it should take. They argued over whether there should be a president (the alternative being an executive committee), whether a bill of rights was needed, whether the slave trade should be outlawed, and numerous other issues.

No matter which of these issues was under debate, the opposing sides usually broke down along Federalist and Anti-Federalist lines. Generally speaking, the Federalists urged the creation of a strong, centralized, federal government. This was necessary, they argued, to regulate trade for all the states, to put down rebellions in the states, to pay war debts, to control a national money supply, and so forth. In contrast, the Anti-Federalists, who were probably in the majority at first, were wary of giving too much power to a centralized national government. Most agreed that such a government was necessary; but in their view it should not overshadow the local authority of each state. In the words of noted historian Merrill Jensen:

> The attachment of citizens to their states was deep and was expressed in the state constitutions. The idea that each colonial government was independent of all outside control had been dinned into American ears ever since 1763. . . . The majority of people . . . agreed that there must be a central government, but they did not want a government that could interfere with either the states or their citizens. They wanted, in fact, a government subordinate to the states and controlled by them. . . . They agreed with eighteenth-century English writers, such as James Burgh, that political power had a dangerous impact on the minds and behavior of men in office [and] that the possession of power created the desire for even more power.[1]

Problems with the Articles

Indeed, such reluctance to grant too much power to a centralized government had been a guiding force behind the framing of the Articles of Confederation, drafted during the American Revolution. A brief examination of the articles and their weaknesses demonstrates two important points. First, the very fact that the articles were structured as they were shows that Anti-Federalist sentiments were strong in the struggling infant nation; second, the inherent weaknesses in the articles, as written, were bound to strengthen the Federalists' case that a stronger federal government was needed.

On paper at least, the articles provided Congress with a wide array of powers. In actual practice, however, its members were often unable to exercise those powers effectively. For example, Congress ostensibly had the authority to declare war and raise and equip armies, to build and equip a navy, to mint and regulate the value of coins, to issue paper money, to borrow money, to establish weights and measures, and to settle disputes among the states. However, under the articles Congress lacked the authority to regulate trade and to raise any moneys except those it requested directly from the states. Put simply, without money Congress could not implement most of the measures it passed. In a widely read 1786 article, a political pundit derided the articles, declaring:

> By this political compact, the United States in congress have exclusive power for the following purposes, without being able to execute one of them. They may make and conclude treaties; but can only recommend the observance of them. They may appoint ambassadors; but cannot defray even the expenses of their tables. They may borrow money in their own name on the faith of the Union; but cannot pay a dollar. They may coin money; but they cannot purchase an ounce of [gold] bullion. They may make war, and determine what number of troops are necessary; but cannot raise a single soldier. *In short, they may declare every thing but do nothing.*[2]

Another weakness of the articles was that they did not provide for a chief executive to oversee the general administration of the government. Congress created new policies and laws, but it had to assign some of its own members to carry them out, a process that turned out to be too disorderly and slow. In an August 1787 letter to a colleague, Edward Carrington, Thomas Jefferson complained:

> Nothing is so embarrassing nor so mischievous in a great assembly as the details of execution. The smallest trifle of that

kind occupies as long as the most important act of legislation, and takes place of every thing else. Let any man recollect, or look over the files of Congress, he will observe the most important propositions hanging over from week to week and month to month, till the occasions have past them, and the thing never done. I have ever viewed the executive details as the greatest cause of evil to us, because they in fact place us as if we had no federal head, by diverting the attention of that head from great to small objects; and should this division of power not be recommended by the Convention, it is my opinion Congress should make it itself by establishing an Executive committee.[3]

Still another shortcoming of the Articles of Confederation was that under its provisions no person had to obey a law made by Congress unless his or her state chose to enforce it. It has been pointed out that this state of affairs stemmed partly from deep-seated feelings of states' rights and the desire to maintain the integrity of local authority. Another factor that made many American leaders reluctant to invest too much authority in the articles was their unhappy dealings with the British Parliament in the years leading up to the American Revolution. As New York University scholar Bernard Schwartz puts it:

> The colonists were unready to concede to Congress powers which they had so strongly refused to Parliament. This was particularly true of the power to tax and the commerce power [i.e., the power to regulate trade for all the states]. The pre-revolutionary experience had instilled in them the belief that such powers should be exercised only by their own local assemblies.[4]

The Constitutional Convention

As a result of the obvious deficiencies of the Articles of Confederation, increasing numbers of the founders came to feel that the articles needed to be drastically overhauled. Among the more prominent members of this group were James Madison, George Washington, and Alexander Hamilton. In their view, the states needed to appoint representatives to convene a national conven-

George Washington presents his ideas for the Articles of Confederation at the Constitutional Convention.

tion with the purpose of scrutinizing, debating, and revising the articles. To that end, the Continental Congress authorized a convention to be held in Philadelphia beginning in May 1787. Eventually fifty-five delegates representing twelve of the thirteen original states attended. Fearing that a more centralized form of government might interfere with local rights and privileges, Rhode Island's legislators refused to send delegates. (These men later overcame their trepidation and became involved in the constitutional process.) The Rhode Island legislators were not the only ones to avoid the convention. Many leading politicians with Anti-Federalist leanings from other states, including Virginia's famous orator and patriot Patrick Henry, stayed home.

This boycott turned out to be a mistake, the effects of which the Anti-Federalists were never able to overcome. Because so many leaders with Federalist leanings did initially attend the convention, they managed to dominate the proceedings. Spearheaded by Madison and Hamilton, who were avid proponents of a strong national government, these men decided to scrap the articles altogether and draft a completely new constitution. Indeed, Madison was leaning this way well before the convention, as revealed in a letter he penned that spring. "No money is paid into the public Treasury," he said in reference to the difficulties created by the weakness of the articles.

> No respect is paid to the federal authority. Not a single State complies with the requisitions [submitted by Congress]; several pass them over in silence, and some positively reject them. . . . It is not possible that a government can last long under these circumstances. If the approaching convention should not agree on some remedy, I am persuaded that some very different arrangement will ensue. The late turbulent scenes in Mass[achuset]ts & infamous ones in Rhode Island, have done inexpressible injury to the republican [democratic] character in that part of the U[nited] States; and a propensity towards Monarchy is said to have been produced by it in some leading minds. . . . I hope the danger of it will rouse all the real friends of the Revolution to exert themselves in favor of such an organization of the confederacy as will perpetuate the Union, and redeem the honor of the Republican name.[5]

Madison's intent was clearly to draft a new constitution that would create a stronger central government. Yet he by no means wanted that government to be so powerful that it trampled on the cherished rights of the states. He foresaw instead a system in which the states and central government shared power in an equitable manner. There must be checks and balances, he reasoned, not only between the national government and the state governments but also between the various branches on the federal level. Some Anti-Federalists, including Pennsylvanian Samuel Bryan, son of court judge George Bryan, argued that instituting such checks and balances would not ensure liberty; only the will of an empowered people could do that. But Madison remained steadfast in his belief that checks and balances were necessary to keeping one branch of the government from becoming tyrannical. He wrote:

> The security against a gradual concentration of the several powers in the same department, consists in giving to those who administer each department, the necessary constitutional means, and personal motives, to resist encroachments [power grabs] of the others. . . . Ambition must be made to counter-

act ambition. . . . In framing a government which is to be administered by men over men, the great difficulty lies in this: You must first enable the government to control the governed; and in the next place, oblige it to control itself.[6]

This classic statement of the virtues of balanced democratic government was first printed in New York's *Independent Journal* and other major newspapers under the pen name Publius. Madison, Hamilton, and fellow Federalist John Jay wrote several other articles under the same name, all intended to rally support for writing a stronger constitution. These essays were later collected as the *Federalist Papers* and universally acclaimed as one of the greatest democratic documents ever written.

Debate over the Bill of Rights

Madison and other supporters of the new constitution were pleased when the Constitutional Convention endorsed the need for such a document. They also saw it as both necessary and healthy for the leading political and legal issues of the day to be hotly debated in anticipation of addressing them in the document's provisions. The need for checks and balances and the form they might take were addressed, as expected; and the delegates argued over whether the nation should have a chief executive. In addition, the slave trade, always a contentious issue, was discussed. Because slavery was so entrenched in the South, especially in Georgia, North Carolina, and South Carolina, the proslavery side won, at least for the moment. A compromise prevented the government from prohibiting the trade before 1809, then more than two decades in the future.

Although Madison had anticipated these and other similar debates, he was surprised when another issue he deemed less pressing became especially divisive. This was the question of whether the Constitution should include a bill of rights—a stated list of civil liberties possessed by all Americans. The Articles of Confederation had no bill of rights. But at the time that document had been drafted most of the founders felt this was not a serious omission. In their view, the individual bills of rights adopted by most of the states were adequate. The first of the original colonies to en-act such a bill was Virginia, on June 12, 1776. (The main author of the document was a popular local legislator named George Mason, whose ideas and writing style had a significant influence on Jefferson during the drafting of the Declaration of Independence.) In addition to the states' bills of rights, Madison reasoned, the Constitution's provisions for separation of powers and a system of checks and balances seemed sufficient safeguards against despotism. So a separate bill of rights on the federal level appeared to be unnecessary.

Nevertheless, many Anti-Federalists lobbied hard to include a bill of rights in the new Constitution. And as the months went by, Madison and many of his Federalist colleagues began to change their minds. Jefferson and Adams both began to advocate inclusion of a constitutional civil rights declaration. In a December 1787 letter, Jefferson rather bluntly told Madison:

> I will now tell you what I do not like [about the new Constitution]. First, the omission of a bill of rights, providing clearly . . . for freedom of religion, freedom of the press, protection against standing armies, restriction of monopolies, the eternal and unremitting force of the habeas corpus laws, and trials by jury in all matters of fact triable by the laws of the land, and not by the laws of nations. . . . I have a right to nothing which another has the right to take away; and [if we do not have a bill of rights] Congress will have a right to take away trials by jury in all civil cases. Let me add that a bill of rights is what the people are entitled to against every government on earth, general or particular; and what no just government should refuse, or rest on inference.[7]

Another reason that Madison changed his mind about a bill of rights for the Constitution was his need to attain some workable level of compromise with Anti-Federalists like Patrick Henry. Madison reasoned correctly that backing a bill of rights would help sell the whole Constitution to Henry and others who doubted the need for such a document in the first place. Eventually, therefore, Madison announced that a bill of rights would satisfy "the minds of well-meaning opponents," and provide extra safeguards to American freedom. "It is my sincere opinion," he stated,

that the Constitution ought to be revised and that the first
Congress meeting under it, ought to prepare and recommend
to the States for ratification, the most satisfactory provisions
for all essential rights, particularly the rights of Conscience in
the fullest latitude, the freedom of the press, trials by jury, security against general warrants, etc.[8]

Madison's compromise not only satisfied most of the Anti-
Federalists, but also, as he had hoped, ensured that the Constitution would be ratified by the states. Henry, Mason, and their fellow Anti-Federalists agreed to ratify the document on the
condition that Madison and the other Federalists would promise
to draft a bill of rights and attach it to the Constitution as soon as
possible. Following these guidelines, in December 1787 Delaware
became the first state to ratify. As the other states followed suit, several of them submitted proposed articles for the rights declaration.
A total in excess of two hundred such amendments were suggested;
and these became the raw material for the process of creating a federal bill of rights that Congress undertook in the summer of 1789.

Ratification and a Legacy of Controversy

The new Constitution could not take effect until at least nine of
the thirteen states ratified it. When New Hampshire became the
ninth state to do so on June 21, 1788, the document officially took
force. The remaining four states ratified it between 1788 and 1790.

This did not end the debates and controversy about the U.S.
Constitution, however. In the ensuing years, lawmakers and ordinary citizens alike periodically reexamined it and argued over
what many saw as glaring omissions and other shortcomings.
Consequently, new constitutional conventions were convened to
amend the document. Each addition sparked further controversy,
both during and after its adoption. The Thirteenth Amendment,
passed shortly after the conclusion of the Civil War, for example,
finally did away with slavery. But much of the discrimination
against blacks remained and, to the dismay of many, was yet to be
addressed by the Constitution. Similarly, the Fifteenth Amendment ensured voting rights for all male citizens regardless of race,
but did not address the issue of women's suffrage. (After much

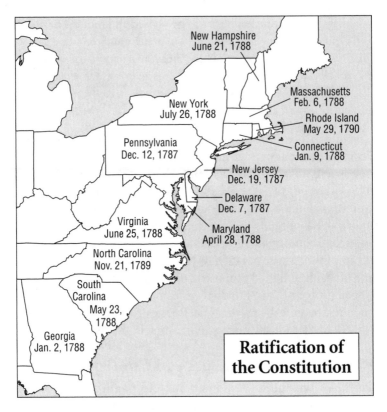

New Hampshire
June 21, 1788

Massachusetts
Feb. 6, 1788

New York
July 26, 1788

Rhode Island
May 29, 1790

Pennsylvania
Dec. 12, 1787

Connecticut
Jan. 9, 1788

New Jersey
Dec. 19, 1787

Delaware
Dec. 7, 1787

Virginia
June 25, 1788

Maryland
April 28, 1788

North Carolina
Nov. 21, 1789

South
Carolina
May 23,
1788

Georgia
Jan. 2, 1788

**Ratification of
the Constitution**

struggle and controversy, the Nineteenth Amendment finally gave women the vote.) Also, many Americans complained that the Constitution did not allow them to vote for the senators who represented them in Congress; this was addressed by the Seventeenth Amendment, which provided for popular election of senators. And so it went.

In the vast majority of these cases, the very act of amending the Constitution was, and remains, controversial and divisive. Some Americans feel that the nation's blueprint for government and civil rights should not be changed except in the most dire circumstances. Others are more willing to amend the document more often to implement their own political, social, economic, or religious agendas. Either way, the stakes involved are enormous; any change in the Constitution inevitably affects the lives of people at all levels of society. It is not merely some archaic, crumbling relic rest-ing in a glass case in a museum, but also in a very real sense a living entity that grows and matures as society grows and matures. In a multitude of ways, the Constitution defines and speaks for the millions of Americans who *are* society. For this and other reasons, the document, its amendments, its creators, and their intent will always be controversial.

Notes

1. Merrill Jensen, *The Making of the American Constitution.* New York: Van Nostrand, 1964, pp. 23–24.
2. Quoted in Bernard Schwartz, *The Reins of Power: A Constitutional History of the United States.* New York: Hill and Wang, 1963, p. 26.
3. Quoted in Julian P. Boyd, ed., *The Papers of Thomas Jefferson*, 60 vols. (projected). Princeton, NJ: Princeton University Press, 1950– , vol. 11, pp. 678–79.
4. Schwartz, *Reins of Power*, p. 27.
5. Quoted in Galliard Hunt, ed., *The Writings of James Madison, 1783–1787*, 9 vols. New York: G.P. Putnam's Sons, 1901, vol. 2, pp. 319–20.
6. James Madison, "Open Letter to the People of the State of New York, from Publius," *Independent Journal*, February 6, 1788.
7. Quoted in Adrienne Koch and William Peden, eds., *The Life and Selected Writings of Thomas Jefferson.* New York: Random House, 1944, pp. 437–38.
8. Quoted in Robert A. Rutland, *James Madison: Founding Father.* New York: Macmillan, 1987, p. 47.

CHAPTER 1

The Need for a Federal Constitution

✳ Chapter Preface

Among the major arguments and debates leading up to the drafting of the U.S. Constitution was whether or not such a document was even needed. Some of the founding fathers felt that the Articles of Confederation, the federal plan adopted by the patriots in 1777, was adequate for the new nation's needs. Others viewed the articles as decidedly inadequate and ineffective; and that has become the judgment of posterity. The subsequent history of the country has shown that the Constitution, which officially replaced the Articles of Confederation in 1787 (pending ratification by the states), is considerably more balanced and effective than the articles. Thus, in retrospect, the few years in which the new nation was governed by the articles constituted a temporary, formative period in which the founders conceived and crafted something better—namely the Constitution.

However, a number of historians and other later observers have pointed out that the articles were not by any means wholly without merit. They did provide a workable basis for a strong central government. And perhaps if they had been easier to amend, the founders would have slowly changed them to fit their needs instead of scrapping them in favor of a completely new document. (One provision of the articles was that any changes in them had to be approved by all of the states, a consensus that was extremely difficult to achieve.)

In a more tangible sense, the adoption of the Articles of Confederation did achieve a political and legal accomplishment of major and lasting value. This was the enactment of the Northwest Ordinance in 1787. In the preceding decade, the new states had squabbled over rights to the lands lying west of the Allegheny Mountains and stretching into the Ohio Valley. Americans were beginning to recognize that they would not always be restricted to the eastern seaboard but would eventually expand toward the west. The question was how these undeveloped western lands would be classified and used. Would they remain territories controlled by the states, either individually or collectively? If one state managed to acquire control of a vast land tract, might it not build its own mini-empire and overshadow the other states? Would it not be better to divide up the western lands into new states, each with an equal voice in Congress? Opposing groups debated these questions hotly in the years following the American Revolution.

The Northwest Ordinance, passed under the Articles of Confederation, settled this major early pre-Constitution dispute. The ordinance provided that the lands lying in the Ohio Valley would, when the time was right, be carved up into new states—at least three and no more than five. A precedent was set. In the decades and centuries that followed, all large tracts of land the nation acquired were partitioned into new states after a brief period of territorial status. As one historian puts it, "This was the crucial accomplishment of the pre-Constitution government, which was to enable the nation to grow as a union of equal states, rather than in accordance with traditional imperial principles." Thus, although the new nation clearly needed a strong new constitution, the short-lived government of the Articles of Confederation provided a critical portion of the sound foundation on which the new nation was being erected.

Viewpoint 1

"We are at peace with all the world. . . . The state governments answer the purposes of preserving the peace, and providing for present exigencies."

The Articles of Confederation Are Adequate

Melancton Smith

The following essay was excerpted from a pamphlet published in 1788 by a New York merchant and landowner, Melancton Smith, who was also a member of the Continental Congress from 1785 to 1788. A staunch Anti-Federalist, Smith was wary of giving too much power to the central government. And as these comments reveal, he felt that the Articles of Confederation, though they could do with some fine-tuning, were sufficient for the task of governing the new nation.

It is insisted, that the present situation of our country is such, as not to admit of a delay in forming a new government, or of time sufficient to deliberate and agree upon the amendments

Melancton Smith, "An Address to the People of the State of New-York: Showing the Necessity of Making Amendments to the Constitution, Proposed for the United States, Previous to Its Adoption," *Pamphlets on the Constitution of the United States, Published During Its Discussion by the People, 1787–1788*, edited by Paul L. Ford. Brooklyn: Historical Printing Club, 1888.

which are proper, without involving ourselves in a state of anarchy and confusion.

On this head, all the powers of rhetoric, and arts of description, are employed to paint the condition of this country, in the most hideous and frightful colors. We are told, that agriculture is without encouragement; trade is languishing; private faith and credit are disregarded, and public credit is prostrate; that the laws and magistrates are contemned and set at naught; that a spirit of licentiousness is rampant, and ready to break over every bound set to it by the government; that private embarrassments and distresses invade the house of every man of middling property, and insecurity threatens every man in affluent circumstances: in short, that we are in a state of the most grievous calamity at home, and that we are contemptible abroad, the scorn of foreign nations, and the ridicule of the world. From this high-wrought picture, one would suppose that we were in a condition the most deplorable of any people upon earth. But suffer me, my countrymen, to call your attention to a serious and sober estimate of the situation in which you are placed, while I trace the embarrassments under which you labor, to their true sources. What is your condition? Does not every man sit under his own vine and under his own fig-tree, having none to make him afraid? Does not every one follow his calling without impediments and receive the reward of his well-earned industry? The farmer cultivates his land, and reaps the fruit which the bounty of heaven bestows on his honest toil. The mechanic is exercised in his art, and receives the reward of his labour. The merchant drives his commerce, and none can deprive him of the gain he honestly acquires; all classes and callings of men amongst us are protected in their various pursuits, and secured by the laws in the possession and enjoyment of the property obtained in those pursuits. The laws are as well executed as they ever were, in this or any other country. Neither the hand of private violence, nor the more to be dreaded hand of legal oppression, are reached out to distress us.

The Nation's Ills Caused by War

It is true, many individuals labour under embarrassments, but these are to be imputed to the unavoidable circumstances of

THE NEED FOR A FEDERAL CONSTITUTION

things, rather than to any defect in our governments. We have just emerged from a long and expensive war. During its existence few people were in a situation to increase their fortunes, but many to diminish them. Debts contracted before the war were left unpaid while it existed, and these were left a burden too heavy to be borne at the commencement of peace. Add to these, that when the war was over, too many of us, instead of reassuming our old habits of frugality, and industry, by which alone every country must be placed in a prosperous condition, took up the profuse use of foreign commodities. The country was deluged with articles imported from abroad, and the cash of the country has been sent to pay for them, and still left us labouring under the weight of a huge debt to persons abroad. These are the true sources to which we are to trace all the private difficulties of individuals: But will a new government relieve you from these? The advocates for it have not yet told you how it will do it—And I will venture to pronounce, that there is but one way in which it can be effected, and that is by industry and economy; limit your expences within your earnings; sell more than you buy, and everything will be well on this score. Your present condition is such as is common to take place after the conclusion of a war. Those who can remember our situation after the termination of the war preceding the last, will recollect that our condition was similar to the present, but time and industry soon recovered us from it. Money was scarce, the produce of the country much lower than it has been since the peace, and many individuals were extremely embarrassed with debts; and this happened although we did not experience the ravages, desolations, and loss of property, that were suffered during the late war.

With regard to our public and national concerns, what is there in our condition that threatens us with any immediate danger? We are at peace with all the world; no nation menaces us with war; nor are we called upon by any cause of sufficient importance to attack any nation. The state governments answer the purposes of preserving the peace, and providing for present exigencies. Our condition as a nation is in no respect worse than it has been for several years past. Our public debt has been lessened in various ways, and the western territory, which has been relied upon as a productive fund to discharge the national debt has at length been brought to market, and a considerable part actually applied to its reduction. I mention these things to shew, that there is nothing special, in our present situation, as it respects our national affairs, that should induce us to accept the proffered system, without taking sufficient time to consider and amend it. I do not mean by this, to insinuate, that our government does not stand in need of a reform. It is admitted by all parties, that alterations are necessary in our federal constitution, but the circumstances of our case do by no means oblige us to precipitate this business, or require that we should adopt a system materially defective. We may safely take time to deliberate and amend, without in the meantime hazarding a condition, in any considerable degree, worse than the present.

Viewpoint 2

"Most of the present difficulties of this country arise from the weakness and other defects of our governments."

The Articles of Confederation Are Inadequate

Benjamin Rush

The negative opinion that many of the Founding Fathers had of the Articles of Confederation in the 1780s is reflected in this article published in February 1787 in a Philadelphia magazine, the *American Museum.* The author was Benjamin Rush, a noted doctor who served as physician general for George Washington's troops in the American Revolution. Rush was also a signer of the Declaration of Independence. In the following selection, he argues in favor of a strong central government.

There is nothing more common than to confound the terms of American Revolution with those of the late American war. The American war is over, but this is far from being the case with American Revolution. On the contrary, nothing but the first act of the great drama is closed. It remains yet to establish and per-

Benjamin Rush, address to the people of the United States, Philadelphia, May 1787.

fect our new forms of government; and to prepare the principles, morals, and manners of our citizens for these forms of government after they are established and brought to perfection.

The confederation, together with most of our state constitutions, were formed under very unfavorable circumstances. We had just emerged from a corrupted monarchy. Although we understood perfectly the principles of liberty, yet most of us were ignorant of the forms and combinations of power in republics. Add to this, the British army was in the heart of our country spreading desolation wherever it went; our resentments, of course, were awakened. We detested the British name, and unfortunately refused to copy some things in the administration of justice and power in the British government which have made it the admiration and envy of the world. In our opposition to monarchy, we forgot that the temple of tyranny has two doors. We bolted one of them by proper restraints; but we left the other open, by neglecting to guard against the effects of our own ignorance and licentiousness.

Federal Power Should Be Divided

Most of the present difficulties of this country arise from the weakness and other defects of our governments.

My business at present shall be only to suggest the defects of the confederation. These consist first, in the deficiency of coercive power; second, in a defect of exclusive power to issue paper money and regulate commerce; third, in vesting the sovereign power of the United States in a single legislature; and fourth, in the too frequent rotation of its members.

A convention is to sit soon for the purpose of devising means of obviating part of the two first defects that have been mentioned. But I wish they may add to their recommendations to each state to surrender up to Congress their power of emitting money. In this way a uniform currency will be produced that will facilitate trade and help to bind the states together. Nor will the states be deprived of large sums of money by this means, when sudden emergencies require it; for they may always borrow them, as they did during the war, out of the treasury of Congress. Even a loan office may be better instituted in this way, in each state, than in any other.

The two last defects that have been mentioned are not of less magnitude than the first. Indeed, the single legislature of Congress will become more dangerous, from an increase of power, than ever. To remedy this, let the supreme federal power be divided, like the legislatures of most of our states, into two distinct, independent branches. Let one of them be styled the council of the states and the other the assembly of the states. Let the first consist of a single delegate and the second, of two, three, or four delegates, chosen annually by each state. Let the President be chosen annu-

Benjamin Rush believed that a new form of government was as important to the American Revolution as the war had been.

ally by the joint ballot of both houses; and let him possess certain powers, in conjunction with a privy council, especially the power of appointing most of the officers of the United States. The officers will not only be better, when appointed this way, but one of the principal causes of faction will be thereby removed from Congress. I apprehend this division of the power of Congress will become more necessary, as soon as they are invested with more ample powers of levying and expending public money.

The custom of turning men out of power or office as soon as they are qualified for it has been found to be absurd in practice. Is it virtuous to dismiss a general, a physician, or even a domestic as soon as they have acquired knowledge sufficient to be useful to us for the sake of increasing the number of able generals, skillful physicians, and faithful servants? We do not. Government is a science, and can never be perfect in America until we encourage men to devote not only three years but their whole lives to it. I believe the principal reason why so many men of abilities object to serving in Congress is owing to their not thinking it worth while to spend three years in acquiring a profession which their country immediately afterwards forbids them to follow.

Knowledge Is Important

There are two errors or prejudices on the subject of government in America which lead to the most dangerous consequences.

It is often said "that the sovereign and all other power is seated in the people." This idea is unhappily expressed. It should be, "all power is derived from the people"; they possess it only on the days of their elections. After this, it is the property of their rulers; nor can they exercise or resume it unless it be abused. It is of importance to circulate this idea, as it leads to order and good government.

The people of America have mistaken the meaning of the word sovereignty; hence each state pretends to be sovereign. In Europe, it is applied only to those states which possess the power of making war and peace, of forming treaties and the like. As this power belongs only to Congress, they are the only sovereign power in the United States.

We commit a similar mistake in our ideas of the word independent. No individual state, as such, has any claim to independence. She is independent only in a union with her sister states in congress.

To conform the principles, morals, and manners of our citizens to our republican forms of government, it is absolutely necessary that knowledge of every kind should be disseminated through every part of the United States.

For this purpose, let Congress, instead of laying out $500,000 in building a federal town, appropriate only a fourth of that sum in founding a federal university. In this university let everything connected with government, such as history, the law of nature and nations, the civil law, the municipal laws of our country, and the principles of commerce, be taught by competent professors. Let masters be employed, likewise, to teach gunnery, fortification, and everything connected with defensive and offensive war. . . .

For the purpose of diffusing knowledge, as well as extending the living principle of government to every part of the United States, every state, city, county, village, and township in the Union should be tied together by means of the post office. This is the true non-electric wire of government. It is the only means of conveying heat and light to every individual in the federal commonwealth. "Sweden lost her liberties," says the Abbé Raynal, "because her citizens were so scattered that they had no means of acting in concert with each other." It should be a constant injunction to the postmasters to convey newspapers free of all charge for postage. They are not only the vehicles of knowledge and intelligence but the sentinels of the liberties of our country.

The Collision of Opinions

The conduct of some of those strangers who have visited our country since the peace and who fill the British papers with accounts of our distresses shows as great a want of good sense as it does of good nature. They see nothing but the foundations and walls of the temple of liberty; and yet they undertake to judge of the whole fabric.

Our own citizens act a still more absurd part when they cry out, after the experience of three or four years, that we are not proper materials for republican government. Remember, we assumed these forms of government in a hurry, before we were prepared for them. Let every man exert himself in promoting virtue and knowledge in our country, and we shall soon become good republicans. Look at the steps by which governments have been changed or rendered stable in Europe. Read the history of Great Britain. Her boasted government has risen out of wars and rebellions that lasted above 600 years. The United States are traveling peaceably into order and good government. They know no strife but what arises from the collision of opinions; and in three years they have advanced further in the road to stability and happiness than most of the nations in Europe have done in as many centuries.

There is but one path that can lead the United States to destruction, and that is their extent of territory. It was probably to effect this that Great Britain ceded to us so much wasteland. But even this path may be avoided. Let but one new state be exposed to sale at a time; and let the land office be shut up till every part of this new state be settled.

I am extremely sorry to find a passion for retirement so universal among the patriots and heroes of the war. They resemble skillful mariners who, after exerting themselves to preserve a ship from sinking in a storm in the middle of the ocean, drop asleep as soon as the waves subside, and leave the care of their lives and property during the remainder of the voyage to sailors without knowledge or experience. Every man in a republic is public property. His time and talents, his youth, his manhood, his old age—nay, more, his life, his all—belong to his country.

Patriots of 1774, 1775, 1776—heroes of 1778, 1779, 1780! Come forward! Your country demands your services! Philosophers and friends to mankind, come forward! Your country demands your studies and speculations! Lovers of peace and order who declined taking part in the late war, come forward! Your country forgives your timidity and demands your influence and advice! Hear her proclaiming, in sighs and groans, in her governments, in her finances, in her trade, in her manufactures, in her morals, and in her manners, "The Revolution is not over!"

Viewpoint 3

"Many important leaders in the eighteenth century did not in fact believe that the majority of ordinary men could govern themselves."

A Number of the Founders Opposed Open Democracy

Merrill Jensen

The divergent motivations of the Founding Fathers are always a topic of debate among scholars and political students. Many people today who examine those motivations are surprised to learn that some of the men who created the Constitution were mistrustful or even openly hostile to the concept of open democracy. In this informative essay, former University of Wisconsin scholar and noted presidential historian Merrill Jensen argues that several of the Federalists who lobbied hard for a strong central government did so in hopes of keeping the country from becoming too democratic.

The overriding constitutional and political result of the American Revolution, both in theory and governmental structure, was an enormous increase in the democratic potential:

Merrill Jensen, *The Making of the American Constitution*. New York: Van Nostrand, 1964. Copyright © 1964 by Merrill Jensen. Reproduced by permission of the publisher.

(1) After 1776 the majority of voters in each state, if agreed upon a program, could put it into effect without any of the internal or external checks provided by British appointed governors, upper houses, and judiciaries, and in the last resort, by the British government in London.

(2) The revolution in theory was absolute, for governments deriving their authority from above were replaced by governments based on the sovereignty of the people, and that idea, however much thwarted in practice, was a potent force that could never again be ignored.

(3) The power of a sovereign central government was replaced by a strictly federal government controlled by the states.

(4) The hierarchy of state officials, most of whom had been appointed before 1776, was replaced by officials who, directly or indirectly, owed their positions to the will of the voters.

(5) The idea that a man was entitled to vote and to hold office because he was a man, and not because he owned a certain amount of property or had a particular religion, made its appearance, and a beginning was made to put it into effect, as was the idea that representation should be according to population and not according to area or to wealth.

After 1776 the sovereign and independent states set about regulating commerce, adopting protective tariffs, encouraging industry, and altering the patterns of taxation. After the war, when a scarcity of money made it difficult for the farmers to pay their private debts and the heavy taxes levied to pay war debts, 7 of the 13 states issued paper money and passed legislation to delay foreclosures on farm mortgages. Paper money, which had been abandoned before the end of the war, was now bitterly opposed by merchants, wealthy planters, and creditors, but the pressure of the farmers, who were the vast majority of the population, was too powerful to be resisted. And when farmers could not get what they wanted from their legislators, they could threaten to use force, as they did in Massachusetts in 1786–1787.

The Opposition to Democracy

Whatever posterity may think, many important leaders in the eighteenth century did not in fact believe that the majority of ordinary men could govern themselves without restraint. They were convinced that democracy had come to America as a result of the American Revolution, and they believed that its coming was evil. They had feared such a result before the Declaration of Independence, and the events in the states during and after the war confirmed their fears. The times were not as bad as some American leaders pictured them, but their dislike of what had happened—and even more, their fear of what might happen—was a real and powerful political force. Hence they worked unceasingly to change the governments created during the revolutionary upheaval. To say this is not to assert that the Founding Fathers were engaged in a "conspiracy," as some naïve writers have charged. Even the slightest acquaintance with the sources reveals that many eighteenth-century leaders did not believe in democracy, either in theory or in practice, and they made no secret of it. They denounced it in private letters, but also in the newspapers, in pamphlets, and in poetry. Furthermore, it should be remembered that in the eighteenth century it was still possible to denounce democracy in public and yet win elections.

Many a colonial leader, as he became a citizen of the new states, scorned the "new men" who rose to power and the "lower orders" who followed them. Thus, Gouverneur Morris in New York decried the "herd of mechanicks" who got military commissions while the gentry were often ignored. Samuel Johnston of North Carolina was shocked because gentlemen were no longer treated with respect. In 1782 a Massachusetts merchant, alarmed at the insecurity of property, wondered who would not fly "to any refuge from anarchy and plebeian despotism?" Jeremy Belknap, a New England clergyman, commented in 1784 that "democratic government" was "to say the least . . . extremely inconvenient." In the same year a South Carolina planter wailed that "gentlemen of property" too often lost elections to the "lower classes." After Shays's Rebellion [in which a group of Massachusetts farmers rebelled against the government] broke out in Massachusetts, Noah Webster, in a widely reprinted newspaper article, announced that he would "definitely prefer a limited monarchy," for he would rather be subject to the "caprice of one man than to the ignorance of a multitude." In 1787 General Henry Knox declared that "a mad democracy sweeps away every moral and divine trait from human character. Hence it is that reason, law, and patriotism is banished from almost every legislature." Perhaps no one summed up the prevailing attitude of the more extreme opponents of democracy better than an army officer who wrote in 1788 that "the philosophy that teaches the equality of mankind and the dignity of human nature is founded in vanity and addressed to it alone . . . there is infinitely more truth in the opposite doctrine that the many were made for the few, and that we are better governed by rods than by reason."

The Demand for a Strong Central Government

The men who deplored what they thought were the democratic results of the Revolution sought to retain control of the state governments, and in some states they were fairly successful. But such control was uncertain at best because of annual elections and legislative supremacy. The other thing they could do (and many of them tried to do it continuously from the beginning of the war) was to create a central government powerful enough to regulate and limit the actions of the states and their citizens. Such men argued that a powerful central government was needed to regulate trade, to control the amount and value of money issued, to suppress rebellions within states, to win the war, to pay the war debts, and the like.

They failed when the Articles of Confederation were written, but as soon as the Articles were ratified, three outstanding and consistent believers in a strong central government—James Madison, James Duane, and James Varnum—were appointed by Congress to propose measures for putting the Confederation into effect. They at once suggested that Congress be given power to impress property in wartime, to appoint tax collectors, and to seize the property of delinquent states. Congress ignored these proposals, which were so contrary to the spirit and the text of the constitution. During the same year Congress proposed an amendment to the Confederation giving it the power to levy import duties. Because of the wartime need for money, 12 states soon approved, but Rhode Island refused the necessary unanimous consent on the grounds that it would alter the character of the central government and endanger liberty. When Virginia joined Rhode Island by repealing her own act of approval, the amendment was killed.

Between 1781 and 1783 Congress was controlled by men who wanted a strong central government, and they argued that the war could not be won without it. But by 1783 the war was won, and in desperation some of them plotted a *coup d'état*. Men like Robert Morris, Gouverneur Morris, and Alexander Hamilton hoped to unite the discontented army officers and the public creditors, and they had the help of generals Henry Knox, Alexander McDougall, Horatio Gates, and lesser army officers. The scheme was for the army to refuse to fight if the war did not end and to refuse to disband if it did. All depended on Washington's leadership, but he killed the scheme in a speech at Newburgh on the Hudson in March 1783.

His action was a striking reversal of what many believed was a lesson of history: that at the end of a successful war the military hero of the war usually took over the government by force and became a dictator in fact if not in name. What Washington's action meant, so far as he and the country were concerned, was that political change must be brought about by political means and not by armed force. His contemporaries, who, unlike posterity, knew their history, knew what they meant when they called him the "American Cincinnatus" [a reference to an ancient Roman leader known for his honesty].

At war's end, defeated at every turn, the proponents of a strong central government continued to try to acquire more power for Congress. Once more they tried to give it the power to collect import duties, and they campaigned hard to give it the power to regulate trade. By 1786 all the states except New York had granted the power to collect duties, and even New York gave a qualified permission, but the power to regulate trade was defeated by the southern planters. They were convinced that this power would result in a monopoly of shipping for the northern merchants, and hence higher freight rates for southern exports, and they would have none of it.

Opposition to a stronger central government had deeper roots.

Robert Morris, as superintendent of finance from 1781 to 1784, had dominated Congress and was the acknowledged leader of those who wanted what was coming to be called a "national government." He had been openly contemptuous of opposition and impatient with constitutional restraints and procedures. His financial program was widely believed to be directed toward enriching himself and his friends at the expense of the country. His methods, his attitudes, and his program . . . alienated even men who sympathized with his ultimate goals. More importantly, he alarmed those revolutionary leaders who clung to the political ideals of 1776. By the 1780's most of them were agreed that the central government must have more power, but they were afraid that men like Morris would undo the basic political and constitutional achievements of the Revolution if they were not blocked. As Richard Henry Lee put it, those who demanded more power for Congress would not rest "until every fence is thrown down that was designed to protect and cover the rights of mankind." And he repeated once more the doctrine that "power poisons the mind of its possessor and aids him to remove the shackles that restrain itself."

Viewpoint 4

"[The] conviction . . . that attempts had been and would be made to establish an aristocracy was shared by a large number of people."

Many of the Founders Opposed Creating an Aristocracy and Dictatorship

Jackson Turner Main

Jackson Turner Main was a professor of history at San Jose State College. Here he delves into some of the deepest fears and worries of those founders who would later become Anti-Federalists as they expressed them during and immediately after the American Revolution. In his view, a majority of them were convinced that there was a danger the future Federalists would impose some sort of military dictatorship based on and intended to perpetuate long-standing aristocratic privileges among men in the upper classes. As Main points out, the formation of a secret society of veteran army officers (the Cincinnati) and other ominous moves by leading Federalists were enough to motivate Anti-Federalists to use any means possible to keep the army from becoming too powerful.

Jackson Turner Main, *The Antifederalists: The Critics of the Constitution, 1781–1788*. Chapel Hill: University of North Carolina Press, 1961. Copyright © 1961 by University of North Carolina Press. Reproduced by permission.

In 1786, the attention of Congress was already turning toward more extensive reforms. The opponents of centralization were not unwilling to strengthen the government under the Articles of Confederation, but they continued to be skeptical of any radical change and suspected the motives of those who advocated it. This suspicious attitude was illustrated in 1785, when the Massachusetts legislature forwarded resolutions to its delegates in Congress recommending a convention to revise the Articles. The delegates replied that a convention would be dangerous, for "plans have been artfully laid, and vigorously pursued, which had they been successful, We think would inevitably have changed our republican Governments into baleful Aristocracies. . . . We are apprehensive and it is our Duty to declare it, that such a Measure would produce thro'out the Union, an Exertion of the Friends of an Aristocracy, to send Members who would promote a Change of Government: and We can form some Judgment of the plan, which such members would report to Congress."

The authors of this reply were neither ignorant nor extremists. Elbridge Gerry, future Antifederalist leader, was a well-to-do merchant; Samuel Holten, Antifederal doctor, ultimately ceased his opposition and withheld his vote in the Massachusetts ratifying convention; and Rufus King was soon to become an ardent Federalist. There were others who shared their opinion. Samuel Osgood had informed John Adams the year before of the danger "that if permanent Funds are given to Congress, the aristocratical Influence, which predominates in more than a Major Part of the United States will finally establish an arbitrary Government in the United States." The same idea often recurs in Stephen Higginson's letters, and in 1787, after he was beginning to change his mind, he wrote, "I sometimes almost lament that the Aristocracy in 1783 was suppressed." This conviction on the part of some well-informed individuals that attempts had been and would be made to establish an aristocracy was shared by a large number of people, and it became a fundamental assumption of the Antifederalists. . . .

Efforts to establish a strong central government had taken various forms. . . . It had been argued that Congress might simply assume powers implied in the Articles or inherent in the nature of any government, and during the last months of the war, some of the Nationalists had tried to use the army to gain their ends. This conspiracy, perhaps more than anything else, excited the fears of future Antifederalists and aroused suspicion of attempts to increase Congress's powers. . . . Finally, the question of constitutional revision was involved in the debate over giving Congress the power to regulate trade. The last two issues require fuller discussion.

Congress and Pensions

The Articles of Confederation registered the general fear of standing armies. Congress was prohibited from maintaining a peacetime force except for internal defense. In war, Congress requested the states to provide troops, which were taken under Congressional direction, but all officers below the rank of general were appointed by the states, and the taxes necessary to support an army were, of course, levied by the states. Even this degree of restriction was not enough to appease some foes of centralization, and their fears were aroused in 1780, when, in order to forestall a mass resignation of military officers, Congress promised half-pay pensions for life to those who would remain in service for the war's duration. This act was widely censured, particularly in New England, and Congress did nothing to redeem the promise until 1788, when . . . the half-pay for life was "commuted" into a grant of five years' full pay. Congress lacked funds to honor this commitment, but the impost of 1783, along with a supplementary fund to be raised by state taxes, which Congress also requested at this time, was expected to provide the money to take care of all federal debts. The impost and the whole question of increasing federal powers therefore became entangled with the dispute over commutation, and matters were further complicated by the formation of the Society of Cincinnati, an hereditary, secret organization of veteran army officers. The Cincinnati was widely suspected of a design to create a permanent nobility and exert political influence—Antifederalists were later to accuse the Society of deliberately fomenting Shays's Rebellion [a revolt by Massachusetts farmers against the government] as part of a deep plot to overturn the government. It was known, at least, that in 1783 some of the officers of the army had conspired with members of Congress in an attempt to force the states to grant federal taxes.

Future Antifederalists were prominent among those who feared the army's political power and opposed military pensions or any other measure which would differentiate the army from the general body of the population and perhaps contribute to the formation of a military caste. In South Carolina, Judge Aedanus Burke led the attack on the Cincinnati. In Massachusetts, half-pay and commutation were supported by the seacoast towns, but the interior was so much opposed that passage of the impost was greatly delayed.

A Dangerous Precedent?

The most extensive and interesting controversy occurred in Connecticut, where the officers were accused of attempting to profit at the expense of the people, who had contributed as much as they had to the war and were suffering equally from the depression. In 1783 the citizens of Killingworth took note of the dangerous game which some of the Nationalists had been playing with the army: "every one must naturally infer that Congress were greatly engaged to get funds . . . in some way and manner, not fixed and established by the articles of confederation—and for that reason, were disposed to secure the interest and influence of the army to effect it." It was argued that Congress did not have power to grant pensions, and that to permit it to assume such a power would establish a dangerous precedent. Powers not specifically granted to Congress remained with the people, from whose ultimate authority there was no appeal, and for Congress to grant a pension was "unconstitutional, unjust and oppressive." The town of Norwich warned its delegates that the people could not escape God's "Just Resentment" if they delegated such control over property to men "so far out of our Reach." Most comprehensive of all was the protest of Farmington. After noting the expense and the unfair discrimination in favor of officers, the town condemned commutation:

Because it is founded on Principles Subertive of a Republican Government Tending to Destroy that Equallity among the citisans which [is] the only permanent foundation on which it can be supported to throw an excessive Power, the constant attendent of property into the Hands of the Few, to cherish those antirepublican Principles & feelings which are now predominent in many of the states, and finally to dissolve our present Happy and

Benevolent Constitution & to erect on the Ruins, a proper Aristocracy: wherein the Body of the People are excluded from all share in the Government, and the Direction & mannagement of the state is committed to the Great & Powerful alone.

Unwilling to trust their legislature, the anti-commutation men resorted to the familiar method of a convention, which met in Middletown in September 1783. The convention stated its purpose to conduct "the most candid and thorough enquiry into the nature, extent and power of Congress" and to determine whether those powers had been exceeded. Since representatives of only twenty-eight towns appeared, it was decided to adjourn in order to give other towns more time to appoint delegates. The convention reassembled in November with a majority of towns in the state present. A petition condemning commutation was sent to the legislature, and a standing committee appointed which was headed by Captain Hugh Ledlie of Hartford and composed, incidentally, mostly of officers. Another meeting was held in March 1784. The delegates repeated their criticism of commutation, attacked the Cincinnati, and favored passage of a bill to pay the state and federal debts by a state impost. The convention planned to meet again, but now opinion was changing. Newspapers were almost universally hostile to further conventions; Samuel Adams responded to an appeal to speak out against them; the impost passed, and the controversy came to an end. In Connecticut, as elsewhere in New England, the anti-commutation feeling was strongest in the interior of the state, in the agricultural upland villages, so many of which were soon to oppose the Constitution.

CHAPTER 2

What Provisions Should the Constitution Have?

✵ Chapter Preface

The framers of the U.S. Constitution got their ideas for the provisions of that document from many diverse sources. But they were especially influenced by a group of progressive seventeenth- and eighteenth-century European political philosopher-writers. These thinkers were part of an important intellectual movement that became known as the European Enlightenment. Their specific ideas differed, but in general they appealed to and celebrated human reason, newly discovered scientific facts, religious tolerance, the existence of certain basic natural human rights, and implementation of fair government. The Enlightenment thinkers believed that the march of science might eventually reveal the true nature of the world; humans could then, in essence, reshape, control, and exploit the world to their advantage. In their view, a crucial portion of this intellectual rebirth was a new understanding of human nature, emphasizing certain inherent rights, including freedom of thought, the right of self-expression, and individual personal fulfillment.

Most of the founding fathers, who were also the framers of the Constitution, took these enlightened concepts to heart. For example, they agreed with English philosopher John Locke (1632–1704) when he criticized rule by the divine right of kings and advocated that government should be based on the consent of the governed. The main function of government, said Locke, should be to preserve people's natural, or God-given, rights, including life, liberty, and property.

One of the more important provisions of the U.S. Constitution—the separation and balance of powers—was inspired by another major Enlightenment figure. Like Locke, French historian and jurist Charles-Louis de Montesquieu (1689–1755) had considered ways to avoid or restrain the excesses of tyrannical government. In his 1748 masterwork *The Spirit of the Laws*, Montesquieu held that a just government must be divided into three fully independent parts or branches—the legislative, executive, and judicial. "When legislative power is united with executive

power in a single person or in a single body of the magistracy,
there is no liberty," he wrote,

> because one can fear that the same monarch or senate that
> makes tyrannical laws will execute them tyrannically. Nor is
> there liberty if the power of judging is not separate from leg-
> islative power and from executive power. If it were joined to
> legislative power, the power over the life and liberty of the cit-
> izens would be arbitrary, for the judge would be the legislator.
> If it were joined to executive power, the judge could have the
> force of an oppressor. All would be lost if the same man or the
> same body of principal men . . . exercised these three powers,
> that of making laws, that of executing public resolutions, and
> that of judging the crimes or the disputes of individuals.

The provisions for separation of powers placed in the Constitution by the American founders, which created an effective system
of political and legal checks and balances, were directly inspired
by these words by Montesquieu. This shows clearly how the
framers took the best ideas of others and adapted them to the existing American situation.

Viewpoint 1

"Ambition must be made to counteract ambition."

A System of Checks and Balances Is Vital

James Madison

As they began to debate the various issues involved in the creation of a new constitution, a number of the delegates to the Constitutional Convention argued that the new government must have a well-thought-out system of checks and balances. Otherwise, one branch of the government might sooner or later become too powerful and overshadow the others. One of the strongest proponents of checks and balances was Virginia's James Madison, often called the "father" of the Constitution for his many contributions to its making. The following tract, in which he explains why checks and balances are necessary, became the fifty-first essay in the famous *Federalist Papers*, a collection authored by Madison, Alexander Hamilton, and John Jay.

*T*o the People of the State of New York.
To what expedient then shall we finally resort for maintaining in practice the necessary partition of power among the several departments, as laid down in the constitution? The only answer that can be given is, that as all these exterior provisions are

James Madison, "Open Letter to the People of the State of New York, from Publius," *Independent Journal*, February 6, 1788.

found to be inadequate, the defect must be supplied, by so contriving the interior structure of the government, as that its several constituent parts may, by their mutual relations, be the means of keeping each other in their proper places. Without presuming to undertake a full developement of this important idea, I will hazard a few general observations, which may perhaps place it in a clearer light, and enable us to form a more correct judgment of the principles and structure of the government planned by the convention.

In order to lay a due foundation for that separate and distinct exercise of the different powers of government, which to a certain extent, is admitted on all hands to be essential to the preservation of liberty, it is evident that each department should have a will of its own; and consequently should be so constituted, that the members of each should have as little agency as possible in the appointment of the members of the others. Were this principle rigorously adhered to, it would require that all the appointments for the supreme executive, legislative, and judiciary magistracies, should be drawn from the same fountain of authority, the people, through channels, having no communication whatever with one another. Perhaps such a plan of constructing the several departments would be less difficult in practice than it may in contemplation appear. Some difficulties however, and some additional expence, would attend the execution of it. Some deviations therefore from the principle must be admitted. In the constitution of the judiciary department in particular, it might be inexpedient to insist rigorously on the principle; first, because peculiar qualifications being essential in the members, the primary consideration ought to be to select that mode of choice, which best secures these qualifications; secondly, because the permanent tenure by which the appointments are held in that department, must soon destroy all sense of dependence on the authority conferring them.

It is equally evident that the members of each department should be as little dependent as possible on those of the others, for the emoluments annexed to their offices. Were the executive magistrate, or the judges, not independent of the legislature in this particular, their independence in every other would be merely nominal.

Ambition Must Counteract Ambition

But the great security against a gradual concentration of the several powers in the same department, consists in giving to those who administer each department, the necessary constitutional means, and personal motives, to resist encroachments of the others. The provision for defence must in this, as in all other cases, be made commensurate to the danger of attack. Ambition must be made to counteract ambition. The interest of the man must be connected with the constitutional rights of the place. It may be a reflection on human nature, that such devices should be necessary to controul the abuses of government. But what is government itself but the greatest of all reflections on human nature? If men were angels, no government would be necessary. If angels were to govern men, neither external nor internal controuls on government would be necessary. In framing a government which is to be administered by men over men, the great difficulty lies in this: You must first enable the government to controul the governed; and in the next place, oblige it to controul itself. A dependence on the people is no doubt the primary controul on the government; but experience has taught mankind the necessity of auxiliary precautions.

This policy of supplying by opposite and rival interests, the defect of better motives, might be traced through the whole system of human affairs, private as well as public. We see it particularly displayed in all the subordinate distributions of power; where the constant aim is to divide and arrange the several offices in such a manner as that each may be a check on the other; that the private interest of every individual, may be a centinel over the public rights. These inventions of prudence cannot be less requisite in the distribution of the supreme powers of the state.

But it is not possible to give to each department an equal power of self defence. In republican government the legislative authority, necessarily, predominates. The remedy for this inconveniency is, to divide the legislature into different branches; and to render them by different modes of election, and different principles of action, as little connected with each other, as the nature of their common functions, and their common dependence on the society, will admit. It may even be necessary to guard against danger-

ous encroachments by still further precautions. As the weight of
the legislative authority requires that it should be thus divided, the
weakness of the executive may require, on the other hand, that it
should be fortified. An absolute negative, on the legislature, appears at first view to be the natural defence with which the executive magistrate should be armed. But perhaps it would be nei-

*James Madison supported the idea of checks and balances to ensure that one
branch of the government did not overpower the others.*

ther altogether safe, nor alone sufficient. On ordinary occasions, it might not be exerted with the requisite firmness; and on extraordinary occasions, it might be perfidiously abused. May not this defect of an absolute negative be supplied, by some qualified connection between this weaker department, and the weaker branch of the stronger department, by which the latter may be led to support the constitutional rights of the former, without being too much detached from the rights of its own department?

If the principles on which these observations are founded be just, as I persuade myself they are, and they be applied as a criterion, to the several state constitutions, and to the federal constitution, it will be found, that if the latter does not perfectly correspond with them, the former are infinitely less able to bear such a test.

The Rights of the Minority

There are moreover two considerations particularly applicable to the federal system of America, which place that system in a very interesting point of view.

First. In a single republic, all the power surrendered by the people, is submitted to the administration of a single government; and usurpations are guarded against by a division of the government into distinct and separate departments. In the compound republic of America, the power surrendered by the people, is first divided between two distinct governments, and then the portion allotted to each, subdivided among distinct and separate departments. Hence a double security arises to the rights of the people. The different governments will controul each other; at the same time that each will be controuled by itself.

Second. It is of great importance in a republic, not only to guard the society against the oppression of its rulers; but to guard one part of the society against the injustice of the other part. Different interests necessarily exist in different classes of citizens. If a majority be united by a common interest, the rights of the minority will be insecure. There are but two methods of providing against this evil: The one by creating a will in the community independent of the majority, that is, of the society itself; the other by comprehending in the society so many separate descriptions of citizens, as will render an unjust combination of a majority of the whole, very improbable, if not impracticable. The first method prevails in all governments possessing an hereditary or self appointed authority. This at best is but a precarious security; because a power independent of the society may as well espouse the unjust views of the major, as the rightful interests, of the minor party, and may possibly be turned against both parties. The second method will be exemplified in the federal republic of the United States. Whilst all authority in it will be derived from and dependent on the society, the society itself will be broken into so many parts, interests and classes of citizens, that the rights of individuals or of the minority, will be in little danger from interested combinations of the majority. In a free government, the security for civil rights must be the same as for religious rights. It consists in the one case in the multiplicity of interests, and in the other, in the multiplicity of sects. The degree of security in both cases will depend on the number of interests and sects; and this may be presumed to depend on the extent of country and number of people comprehended under the same government. This view of the subject must particularly recommend a proper federal system to all the sincere and considerate friends of republican government: Since it shews that in exact proportion as the territory of the union may be formed into more circumscribed confederacies or states, oppressive combinations of a majority will be facilitated, the best security under the republican form, for the rights of every class of citizens, will be diminished; and consequently, the stability and independence of some member of the government, the only other security, must be proportionally increased.

Justice and the General Good

Justice is the end of government. It is the end of civil society. It ever has been, and ever will be pursued, until it be obtained, or until liberty be lost in the pursuit. In a society under the forms of which the stronger faction can readily unite and oppress the weaker, anarchy may as truly be said to reign, as in a state of nature where the weaker individual is not secured against the violence of the stronger: And as in the latter state even the stronger individuals are prompted by the uncertainty of their condition, to submit to a government which may protect the weak as well as themselves: So in the former state, will the more powerful factions or parties be gradually induced by a like motive, to wish for a government which will protect all parties, the weaker as well as the more powerful. It can be little doubted, that if the state of Rhode Island was separated from the confederacy, and left to itself, the insecurity of rights under the popular form of government within such narrow limits, would be displayed by such reiterated oppressions of factious majorities, that some power altogether independent of the people would soon be called for by the voice of the very factions whose misrule had proved the necessity of it. In the extended republic of the United States, and among the great variety of interests, parties and sects which it embraces, a coalition of a majority of the whole society could seldom take place on any other principles than those of justice and the general good; and there being thus less danger to a minor from the will of the major party, there must be less pretext also, to provide for the security of the former, by introducing into the government a will not dependent on the latter; or in other words, a will independent of the society itself. It is no less certain than it is important, notwithstanding the contrary opinions which have been entertained, that the larger the society, provided it lie within a practicable sphere, the more duly capable it will be of self government. And happily for the *republican cause*, the practicable sphere may be carried to a very great extent, by a judicious modification and mixture of the *federal principle.*

Viewpoint 2

*"If the administrators of every government are
actuated by . . . ambition, how is the welfare . . .
of the community to be the result of such jarring
adverse interests?"*

A System of Checks
and Balances Is Not
Vital

Samuel Bryan

Many early American leaders opposed equipping the new government with a system of checks and balances. They argued that such a system would be necessary only if the government and the Constitution underlying it were overly complex. For example, a Pennsylvanian named Samuel Bryan (son of a prominent judge) wrote the following essay extolling the virtues of the more simple, and in his view elegant, constitution of his state. At the time, Pennsylvania was governed by a popular assembly possessing all governmental powers. The members of the assembly voted for twelve of their number to become executive councilmen, a sort of committee of presidents. Bryan and those who agreed with him argued that if such leaders were virtuous (ostensibly, only the most trustworthy men would be nominated for such high positions) and elected to short terms there would

Samuel Bryan, "To the Freemen of Pennsylvania, from Centinel," *Independent Gazetteer*, October 5, 1787.

be little chance of corruption or tyranny. In such a system, therefore, no elaborate checks and balances would be necessary.

To the Freemen of Pennsylvania.
Friends, Countrymen and Fellow Citizens,
Permit one of yourselves to put you in mind of certain *liberties* and *privileges* secured to you by the constitution of this commonwealth, and to beg your serious attention to his uninterested opinion upon the plan of federal government submitted to your consideration, before you surrender these great and valuable privileges up forever. Your present frame of government, secures to you a right to hold yourselves, houses, papers and possessions free from search and seizure, and therefore warrants granted without oaths or affirmations first made, affording sufficient foundation for them, whereby any officer or messenger may be commanded or required to search your houses or seize your persons or property, not particularly described in such warrant, shall not be granted. Your constitution further provides "that in controversies respecting property, and in suits between man and man, the parties have a right *to trial by jury, which ought to be held sacred.*" It also provides and declares, *"that the people have a right of* FREEDOM OF SPEECH, *and of* WRITING *and* PUBLISHING *their sentiments, therefore* THE FREEDOM OF THE PRESS OUGHT NOT TO BE RESTRAINED." The constitution of Pennsylvania is *yet* in existence, *as yet* you have the right to *freedom of speech*, and of *publishing your sentiments*. How long those rights will appertain to you, you yourselves are called upon to say, whether your *houses* shall continue to be your *castles;* whether your *papers*, your *persons* and your *property*, are to be held sacred and free from *general warrants*, you are now to determine. Whether the *trial by jury* is to continue as your birth-right, the freemen of Pennsylvania, nay, of all America, are now called upon to declare.

Men of High Integrity and Patriotism

Without presuming upon my own judgement, I cannot think it an unwarrantable presumption to offer my private opinion, and call upon others for their's; and if I use my pen with the boldness of a freeman, it is because I know that *the liberty of the press yet remains unviolated*, and *juries yet are judges.*

The late Convention have submitted to your consideration a plan of a new federal government—The subject is highly interesting to your future welfare—Whether it be calculated to promote the great ends of civil society, *viz.* the happiness and prosperity of the community; it behoves you well to consider, uninfluenced by the authority of names. Instead of that frenzy of enthusiasm, that has actuated the citizens of Philadelphia, in their approbation of the proposed plan, before it was possible that it could be the result of a rational investigation into its principles; it ought to be dispassionately and deliberately examined, and its own intrinsic merit the only criterion of your patronage. If ever free and unbiassed discussion was proper or necessary, it is on such an occasion.—All the blessings of liberty and the dearest privileges of freemen, are now at stake and dependent on your present conduct. Those who are competent to the task of developing the principles of government, ought to be encouraged to come forward, and thereby the better enable the people to make a proper judgment; for the science of government is so abstruse, that few are able to judge for themselves; without such assistance the people are too apt to yield an implicit assent to the opinions of those characters, whose abilities are held in the highest esteem, and to those in whose integrity and patriotism they can confide; not considering that the love of domination is generally in proportion to talents, abilities, and superior acquirements; and that the men of the greatest purity of intention may be made instruments of despotism in the hands of the *artful and designing.* If it were not for the stability and attachment which time and habit gives to forms of government, it would be in the power of the enlightened and aspiring few, if they should combine, at any time to destroy the best establishments, and even make the people the instruments of their own subjugation.

The late revolution having effaced in a great measure all former habits, and the present institutions are so recent, that there exists not that great reluctance to innovation, so remarkable in old communities, and which accords with reason, for the most comprehensive mind cannot foresee the full operation of material changes on civil polity; it is the genius of the common law to resist innovation.

The wealthy and ambitious, who in every community think they have a right to lord it over their fellow creatures, have availed themselves, very successfully, of this favorable disposition; for the people thus unsettled in their sentiments, have been prepared to accede to any extreme of government; all the distresses and difficulties they experience, proceeding from various causes, have been ascribed to the impotency of the present confederation, and thence they have been led to expect full relief from the adoption of the proposed system of government; and in the other event, immediately ruin and annihilation as a nation. These characters flatter themselves that they have lulled all distrust and jealousy of their new plan, by gaining the concurrence of the two men in whom America has the highest confidence, and now triumphantly exult in the completion of their long meditated schemes of power and aggrandisement. I would be very far from insinuating that the two illustrious personages alluded to, have not the welfare of their country at heart; but that the unsuspecting goodness and zeal of the one, has been imposed on, in a subject of which he must be necessarily inexperienced, from his other arduous engagements; and that the weakness and indecision attendant on old age, has been practised on in the other.

A Great Disparity of Talents and Wisdom

I am fearful that the principles of government inculcated in Mr. [John] Adams's treatise [*Defence of the Constitutions of Government of the United States*], and enforced in the numerous essays and paragraphs in the newspapers, have misled some well designing members of the late Convention. . . .

I have been anxiously expecting that some enlightened patriot would, ere this, have taken up the pen to expose the futility, and counteract the baneful tendency of such principles. Mr. Adams's *sine qua non* of a good government is three balancing powers, whose repelling qualities are to produce an equilibrium of interests, and thereby promote the happiness of the whole community. He asserts that the administrators of every government, will ever be actuated by views of private interest and ambition, to the prejudice of the public good; that therefore the only effectual method to secure the rights of the people and promote their welfare, is to create an opposition of interests between the members of two distinct bodies, in the exercise of the powers of government, and balanced by those of a third. This hypothesis supposes human wisdom competent to the task of instituting three co-equal orders in government, and a corresponding weight in the community to enable them respectively to exercise their several parts, and whose views and interests should be so distinct as to prevent a coalition of any two of them for the destruction of the third. Mr. Adams, although he has traced the constitution of every form of government that ever existed, as far as history affords materials, has not been able to adduce a single instance of such a government; he indeed says that the British constitution is such in theory, but this is rather a confirmation that his principles are chimerical and not to be reduced to practice. If such an organization of power were practicable, how long would it continue? not a day—for there is so great a disparity in the talents, wisdom and industry of mankind, that the scale would presently preponderate to one or the other body, and with every accession of power the means of further increase would be greatly extended. The state of society in England is much more favorable to such a scheme of government than that of America. There they have a powerful hereditary nobility, and real distinctions of rank and interests; but even there, for want of that perfect equallity of power and distinction of interests, in the three orders of government, they exist but in name; the only operative and efficient check, upon the conduct of administration, is the sense of the people at large.

Suppose a government could be formed and supported on such principles, would it answer the great purposes of civil society; if the administrators of every government are actuated by views of private interest and ambition, how is the welfare and happiness of the community to be the result of such jarring adverse interests?

Imitate Pennsylvania?

Therefore, as different orders in government will not produce the good of the whole, we must recur to other principles. I believe it will be found that the form of government, which holds those entrusted with power, in the greatest responsibility to their constituents, the best calculated for freemen. A republican, or free government, can only exist where the body of the people are virtuous, and where property is pretty equally divided[;] in such a government the people are the sovereign and their sense or opinion is the criterion of every public measure; for when this ceases to be the case, the nature of the government is changed, and an aristocracy, monarchy or despotism will rise on its ruin. The highest responsibility is to be attained, in a simple structure of government, for the great body of the people never steadily attend to the operations of government, and for want of due information are liable to be imposed on—If you complicate the plan by various orders, the people will be perplexed and divided in their sentiments about the source of abuses or misconduct, some will impute it to the senate, others to the house of representatives, and so on, that the interposition of the people may be rendered imperfect or perhaps wholly abortive. But if, imitating the constitution of Pennsylvania, you vest all the legislative power in one body of men (separating the executive and judicial) elected for a short period, and necessarily excluded by rotation from permanency, and guarded from precipitancy and surprise by delays imposed on its proceedings, you will create the most perfect responsibility for them, whenever the people feel a grievance they cannot mistake the authors, and will apply the remedy with certainty and effect, discarding them at the next election. This tie of responsibility will obviate all the dangers apprehended from a single legislature, and will the best secure the rights of the people. . . .

The proposed plan of government . . . has none of the essential requisites of a free government; . . . it is neither founded on those balancing restraining powers, recommended by Mr. Adams and attempted in the British constitution, or possessed of that responsibility to its constituents, which, in my opinion, is the only effectual security for the liberties and happiness of the people; but on the contrary, that it is a most daring attempt to establish a despotic aristocracy among freemen, that the world has ever witnessed.

Viewpoint 3

"Decision, activity, secrecy, and dispatch will generally characterise the proceedings of one man . . . [more] than the proceedings of any greater number."

The Executive Should Be One Person

Alexander Hamilton

Alexander Hamilton, a military aide to George Washington during the Revolutionary War and later secretary of the treasury during Washington's presidency, was one of the main advocates for a stronger national government to replace the Articles of Confederation. A New York delegate to the Constitutional Convention in Philadelphia, Hamilton's role and influence were limited, in part because he was continually outvoted by other members of his own New York delegation. However, he did play a major role in getting the Constitution ratified in New York in 1788.

As part of the ratification effort Hamilton wrote, along with James Madison and John Jay, a series of newspaper articles known as the *Federalist Papers* explaining and supporting the different parts of the new Constitution. The following is taken from *Federalist* No. 70, in which Hamilton defends the office of the president as created by the Constitution. He argues that the need for an "energetic" executive is best served when the executive is a single person. He opposes proposals for a plural execu-

Alexander Hamilton, "Open Letter to the People of the State of New York, from Publius," *Federalist* No. 70, *Independent Journal*, May 1788.

tive or for an executive council that would oversee and share powers with the president.

There is an idea, which is not without its advocates, that a vigorous executive is inconsistent with the genius of republican government. The enlightened well wishers to this species of government must at least hope that the supposition is destitute of foundation; since they can never admit its truth, without at the same time admitting the condemnation of their own principles. Energy in the executive is a leading character in the definition of good government. It is essential to the protection of the community against foreign attacks: It is not less essential to the steady administration of the laws, to the protection of property against those irregular and high handed combinations, which sometimes interrupt the ordinary course of justice, to the security of liberty against the enterprises and assaults of ambition, of faction and of anarchy. Every man the least conversant in Roman story knows how often that republic was obliged to take refuge in the absolute power of a single man, under the formidable title of dictator, as well against the intrigues of ambitious individuals, who aspired to the tyranny, and the seditions of whole classes of the community, whose conduct threatened the existence of all government, as against the invasions of external enemies, who menaced the conquest and destruction of Rome.

There can be no need however to multiply arguments or examples on this head. A feeble executive implies a feeble execution of the government. A feeble execution is but another phrase for a bad execution: And a government ill executed, whatever it may be in theory, must be in practice a bad government.

Taking it for granted, therefore, that all men of sense will agree in the necessity of an energetic executive; it will only remain to inquire, what are the ingredients which constitute this energy— how far can they be combined with those other ingredients which constitute safety in the republican sense? And how far does this combination characterise the plan, which has been reported by the convention?

The ingredients, which constitute energy in the executive, are first unity, secondly duration, thirdly an adequate provision for its support, fourthly competent powers.

The circumstances which constitute safety in the republican sense are, Ist. a due dependence on the people, secondly a due responsibility.

Those politicians and statesmen, who have been the most celebrated for the soundness of their principles, and for the justness of their views, have declared in favor of a single executive and a numerous legislature. They have with great propriety considered energy as the most necessary qualification of the former, and have regarded this as most applicable to power in a single hand; while they have with equal propriety considered the latter as best adapted to deliberation and wisdom, and best calculated to conciliate the confidence of the people and to secure their privileges and interests.

That unity is conducive to energy will not be disputed. Decision, activity, secrecy, and dispatch will generally characterise the proceedings of one man, in a much more eminent degree, than the proceedings of any greater number; and in proportion as the number is increased, these qualities will be diminished.

This unity may be destroyed in two ways; either by vesting the power in two or more magistrates of equal dignity and authority; or by vesting it ostensibly in one man, subject in whole or in part to the controul and co-operation of others, in the capacity of counsellors to him. Of the first the two consuls of Rome may serve as an example; of the last we shall find examples in the constitutions of several of the states. New-York and New-Jersey, if I recollect right, are the only states, which have entrusted the executive authority wholly to single men. Both these methods of destroying the unity of the executive have their partisans; but the votaries of an executive council are the most numerous. They are both liable, if not to equal, to similar objections; and may in most lights be examined in conjunction.

The experience of other nations will afford little instruction on this head. As far however as it teaches any thing, it teaches us not to be inamoured of plurality in the executive. We have seen that the Achæans on an experiment of two Prætors, were induced to abolish one. The Roman history records many instances of mischiefs to the republic from the dissentions between the consuls, and between the military tribunes, who were at times substituted to the consuls. But it gives us no specimens of any peculiar advantages derived to the state, from the circumstance of the plurality of those magistrates. . . .

But quitting the dim light of historical research, and attaching ourselves purely to the dictates of reason and good sense, we shall discover much greater cause to reject than to approve the idea of plurality in the executive, under any modification whatever.

Unnecessary Divisions

Wherever two or more persons are engaged in any common enterprize or pursuit, there is always danger of difference of opinion. If it be a public trust or office in which they are cloathed with equal dignity and authority, there is peculiar danger of personal emulation and even animosity. From either and especially from all these causes, the most bitter dissentions are apt to spring. Whenever these happen, they lessen the respectability, weaken the authority, and distract the plans and operations of those whom they divide. If they should unfortunately assail the supreme executive magistracy of a country, consisting of a plurality of persons, they might impede or frustrate the most important measures of the government, in the most critical emergencies of the state. And what is still worse, they might split the community into the most violent and irreconcilable factions adhering differently to the different individuals who composed the magistracy. . . .

Upon the principles of a free government, inconveniencies from the source just mentioned must necessarily be submitted to in the formation of the legislature; but it is unnecessary and therefore unwise to introduce them into the constitution of the executive. It is here too that they may be most pernicious. In the legislature, promptitude of decision is oftener an evil than a benefit. The differences of opinion, and the jarrings of parties in that department of the government, though they may sometimes obstruct salutary plans, yet often promote deliberation and circumspection; and serve to check excesses in the majority. When a resolution too is once taken, the opposition must be at an end. That resolution is a law, and resistance to it punishable. But no favourable circumstances palliate or atone for the disadvantages of dissention in the executive department. Here they are pure and unmixed. There is no point at which they cease to operate. They serve to embarrass and weaken the execution of the plan or measure, to which they relate, from the first step to the final conclusion of it. They constantly counteract those qualities in the executive, which are the most necessary ingredients in its composition, vigour and expedition, and this without any counterballancing good. In the conduct of war, in which the energy of the executive is the bulwark of the national security, every thing would be to be apprehended from its plurality.

It must be confessed that these observations apply with principal weight to the first case supposed, that is to a plurality of magistrates of equal dignity and authority; a scheme the advocates for which are not likely to form a numerous sect: But they apply, though not with equal, yet with considerable weight, to the project of a council, whose concurrence is made constitutionally necessary to the operations of the ostensible executive. An artful cabal in that council would be able to distract and to enervate the whole system of administration. If no such cabal should exist, the mere diversity of views and opinions would alone be sufficient to tincture the exercise of the executive authority with a spirit of habitual feebleness and dilatoriness.

But one of the weightiest objections to a plurality in the executive, and which lies as much against the last as the first plan, is that it tends to conceal faults, and destroy responsibility. Responsibility is of two kinds, to censure and to punishment. The first is the most important of the two; especially in an elective office. Man, in public trust, will much oftener act in such a manner as to render him unworthy of being any longer trusted, than in such a manner as to make him obnoxious to legal punishment. But the multiplication of the executive adds to the difficulty of detection in either case. It often becomes impossible, amidst mutual accusations, to determine on whom the blame or the punishment of a pernicious measure, or series of pernicious measures ought really to fall. It is shifted from one to another with so much dexterity, and under such plausible appearances, that the public opinion is left in suspense about the real author. The circumstances which may have led to any national miscarriage or misfortune are sometimes so complicated, that where there are a number of actors who may have had different degrees and kinds of agency, though we may clearly see upon the whole that there has been mismanagement, yet it may be impracticable to pronounce to whose account the evil which may have been incurred is truly chargeable.

"I was overruled by my council. The council were so divided in their opinions, that it was impossible to obtain any better resolution on the point." These and similar pretexts are constantly at hand, whether true or false. And who is there that will either take the trouble or incur the odium of a strict scrutiny into the secret springs of the transaction? Should there be found a citizen zealous enough to undertake the unpromising task, if there happen to be a collusion between the parties concerned, how easy is it to cloath the circumstances with so much ambiguity, as to render it uncertain what was the precise conduct of any of those parties? . . .

It is evident from these considerations, that the plurality of the executive tends to deprive the people of the two greatest securities they can have for the faithful exercise of any delegated power; first, the restraints of public opinion, which lose their efficacy as well on account of the division of the censure attendant on bad measures among a number, as on account of the uncertainty on whom it ought to fall; and secondly, the opportunity of discovering with facility and clearness the misconduct of the persons they trust, in order either to their removal from office, or to their actual punishment, in cases which admit of it.

In England the king is a perpetual magistrate; and it is a maxim, which has obtained for the sake of the public peace, that he is unaccountable for his administration, and his person sacred. Nothing therefore can be wiser in that kingdom than to annex to the king a constitutional council, who may be responsible to the nation for the advice they give. Without this there would be no responsibility whatever in the executive department; an idea inadmissible in a free government. But even there the king is not bound by the resolutions of his council, though they are answerable for the advice they give. He is the absolute master of his own conduct, in the exercise of his office; and may observe or disregard the council given to him at his sole discretion.

Against a Council to the Executive

But in a republic, where every magistrate ought to be personally responsible for his behaviour in office, the reason which in the British constitution dictates the propriety of a council not only ceases to apply, but turns against the institution. In the monarchy of Great-Britain, it furnishes a substitute for the prohibited responsibility of the chief magistrate; which serves in some degree as a hostage to the national justice for his good behaviour. In the American republic it would serve to destroy, or would greatly diminish the intended and necessary responsibility of the chief magistrate himself.

The idea of a council to the executive, which has so generally obtained in the state constitutions, has been derived from that maxim of republican jealousy, which considers power as safer in the hands of a number of men than of a single man. If the maxim should be admitted to be applicable to the case, I should contend that the advantage on that side would not counterballance the numerous disadvantages on the opposite side. But I do not think the rule at all applicable to the executive power. I clearly concur in opinion in this particular with a writer whom the celebrated Junius pronounces to be "deep, solid and ingenious," that, "the executive power is more easily confined when it is one": That it is far more safe there should be a single object for the jealousy and watchfulness of the people; and in a word that all multiplication of the executive is rather dangerous than friendly to liberty.

A little consideration will satisfy us, that the species of security sought for in the multiplication of the executive is unattainable. Numbers must be so great as to render combination difficult; or they are rather a source of danger than of security. The united credit and influence of several individuals must be more formidable to liberty than the credit and influence of either of them separately. When power therefore is placed in the hands of so small a number of men, as to admit of their interests and views being easily combined in a common enterprise, by an artful leader, it becomes more liable to abuse and more dangerous when abused, than if it be lodged in the hands of one man; who from the very circumstance of his being alone will be more narrowly watched and more readily suspected, and who cannot unite so great a mass of influence as when he is associated with others. The Decemvirs of Rome, whose name denotes their number [ten], were more to be dreaded in their usurpation than any ONE of them would have been. No person would think of proposing an executive much more numerous than that body, from six to a dozen have been suggested for the number of the council. The extreme of these numbers is not too great for an easy combination; and from such a combination America would have more to fear, than from the ambition of any single individual. A council to a magistrate, who is himself responsible for what he does, are generally nothing better than a clog upon his good intentions; are often the instruments and accomplices of his bad, and are almost always a cloak to his faults.

I forbear to dwell upon the subject of expence; though it be evident that if the council should be numerous enough to answer the principal end, aimed at by the institution, the salaries of the members, who must be drawn from their homes to reside at the seat of government, would form an item in the catalogue of public expenditures, too serious to be incurred for an object of equivocal utility.

I will only add, that prior to the appearance of the constitution, I rarely met with an intelligent man from any of the states, who did not admit as the result of experience, that the UNITY of the Executive of this state was one of the best of the distinguishing features of our constitution.

Viewpoint 4

"If the Executive is vested in three Persons, . . . will it not contribute to quiet the Minds of the People?"

The Executive Should Be a Committee

George Mason

Virginia planter and political leader George Mason was one of the more active delegates at the Constitutional Convention, where he drew on his experience of helping to write Virginia's 1776 state constitution. However, when the Constitution was finished on September 17, 1787, Mason was one of three delegates who refused to sign it, in part because it lacked a bill of rights similar to the one Mason had written for Virginia's constitution.

The following is taken from a speech Mason made on June 4, 1787, when the convention was debating how the executive should be set up in the proposed new government. Mason was generally supportive of James Madison's wishes for a stronger national government with a strong executive, but he feared the potential dangers of creating a new tyrant. In his speech, Mason proposes to prevent such a development by making the executive a committee of three people.

The chief advantages which have been urged in favour of Unity in the Executive, are the Secrecy, the Dispatch, the Vigour and

George Mason, speech to the Constitutional Convention, June 4, 1787.

Energy which the Government will derive from it; especially in time of War. That these are great Advantages, I shall most readily allow. They have been strongly insisted on by all monarchical Writers—they have been acknowledged by the ablest and most candid Defenders of Republican Government; and it can not be denied that a Monarchy possesses them in a much greater Degree than a Republic. Yet perhaps a little Reflection may incline us to doubt whether these advantages are not greater in Theory than in Practice—or lead us to enquire whether there is not some prevailing Principle in Republican Government, which sets at Naught, and tramples upon this boasted Superiority—as hath been experienced, to their cost by most Monarchys, which have been imprudent enough to invade or attack their republican Neighbors. This invincible Principle is to be found in the Love the Affection the Attachment of the Citizens to their Laws, to their Freedom, and to their Country. Every Husbandman will be quickly converted into a Soldier, when he knows and feels that he is to fight not in defence of the Rights of a particular Family, or a Prince; but for his own. This is the true Construction of that pro Aris and focis [for altars and firesides] which has, in all Ages, perform'd such Wonders. It was this which, in ancient times, enabled the little Cluster of Grecian Republics to resist and almost constantly to defeat the Persian Monarch. It was this which supported the States of Holland against a Body of veteran Troops through a Thirty Years War with Spain, then the greatest Monarchy in Europe and finally rendered them victorious. It is this which preserves the Freedom and Independence of the Swiss Cantons, in the midst of the most powerful Nations. And who that reflects seriously upon the Situation of America, in the Beginning of the late War—without Arms—without Soldiers—without Trade, Money, or Credit—in a Manner destitute of all Resources, but must ascribe our Success to this pervading all-powerful Principle?

An Executive of Three Persons

We have not yet been able to define the Powers of the Executive; and however moderately some Gentlemen may talk or think upon the Subject, I believe there is a general Tendency to a strong Executive and I am inclined to think a strong Executive necessary. If strong and extensive Powers are vested in the Executive, and that Executive consists only of one Person, the Government will of course degenerate, (for I will call it degeneracy) into a Monarchy—A Government so contrary to the Genius of the People, that they will reject even the Appearance of it. I consider the federal Government as in some Measure dissolved by the Meeting of this Convention. Are there no Dangers to be apprehended from procrastinating the time between the breaking up of this Assembly and the adoption of a new System of Government. I dread the Interval. If it should not be brought to an Issue in the Course of the first Year, the Consequences may be fatal. Has not the different Parts of this extensive Government, the several States of which it is composed a Right to expect an equal Participation in the Executive, as the best Means of securing an equal Attention to their Interests. Should an Insurrection, a Rebellion or Invasion happen in New Hampshire when the single supreme Magistrate is a Citizen of Georgia, would not the people of New Hampshire naturally ascribe any Delay in defending them to such a Circumstance and so vice versa. If the Executive is vested in three Persons, one chosen from the northern, one from the middle, and one from the Southern States, will it not contribute to quiet the Minds of the People, & convince them that there will be proper attention paid to their respective Concerns? Will not three Men so chosen bring with them, into Office, a more perfect and extensive Knowledge of the real Interests of this great Union? Will not such a Model of Appointment be the most effectual means of preventing Cabals and Intrigues between the Legislature and the Candidates for this Office, especially with those Candidates who from their local Situation, near the seat of the federal Government, will have the greatest Temptations and the greatest Opportunities. Will it not be the most effectual Means of checking and counteracting the aspiring Views of dangerous and ambitious Men, and consequently the best Security for the Stability and Duration of our Government upon the invaluable Principles of Liberty? These Sir, are some of my Motives for preferring an Executive consisting of three Persons rather than of one.

"My mind will not be quieted till I see something substantial come forth in the shape of a Bill of Rights."

The Constitution Needs a Bill of Rights

Patrick Henry

As ratification of the new Constitution loomed, many Anti-Federalists expressed their worries that the document lacked a bill of rights. Perhaps the most prominent of these voices was that of Patrick Henry, the renowned Virginia orator who led the opposition to the Constitution in his home state. The following words come from some of Henry's speeches delivered in 1788, shortly before ratification. He argued that having a bill of rights like the one attached to the Virginia state constitution was necessary to safeguard the freedoms of the American people.

16 June 1788

Mr. Chairman.—The necessity of a Bill of Rights appear to me to be greater in this Government, than ever it was in any Government before. . . .

All nations have adopted this construction—That all rights not expressly and unequivocally reserved to the people, are impliedly

David Robertson, ed., *Debates and Other Proceedings of the Convention of Virginia*. Richmond, VA: Inquirer Press, 1805.

and incidentally relinquished to rulers; as necessarily inseparable from the delegated powers. It is so in Great-Britain: For every possible right which is not reserved to the people by some express provision or compact, is within the King's prerogative. It is so in that country which is said to be in such full possession of freedom. It is so in Spain, Germany, and other parts of the world.

Exposed to the Armed and Powerful?

Let us consider the sentiments which have been entertained by the people of America on this subject. At the revolution, it must be admitted, that it was their sense to put down those great rights which ought in all countries to be held inviolable and sacred. Virginia did so we all remember. She made a compact to reserve, expressly, certain rights. When fortified with full, adequate, and abundant representation, was she satisfied with that representation? No.—She most cautiously and guardedly reserved and secured those invaluable, inestimable rights and privileges, which no people, inspired with the least glow of the patriotic love of liberty, ever did, or ever can, abandon. She is called upon now to abandon them, and dissolve that compact which secured them to her. She is called upon to accede to another compact which most infallibly supercedes and annihilates her present one. Will she do it?—This is the question. If you intend to reserve your unalienable rights, you must have the most express stipulation. For if implication be allowed, you are ousted of those rights. If the people do not think it necessary to reserve them, they will be supposed to be given up. How were the Congressional rights defined when the people of America united by a confederacy to defend their liberties and rights against the tyrannical attempts of Great-Britain? The States were not then contented with implied reservation. No, Mr. Chairman. It was expressly declared in our Confederation that every right was retained by the States respectively, which was not given up to the Government of the United States. But there is no such thing here. You therefore by a natural and unavoidable implication, give up your rights to the General Government. Your own example furnishes an argument against it. If you give up these powers, without a Bill of Rights, you will exhibit the most absurd thing to mankind that ever the world saw—A Government that has abandoned all its powers—The powers of direct taxation, the sword, and the purse. You have disposed of them to Congress, without a Bill of Rights—without check, limitation, or controul. And still you have checks and guards—still you keep barriers— pointed where? Pointed against your weakened, prostrated, ener-vated State Government! You have a Bill of Rights to defend you against the State Government, which is bereaved of all power; and yet you have none against Congress, though in full and exclusive possession of all power! You arm yourselves against the weak and defenceless, and expose yourselves naked to the armed and pow-erful. Is not this a conduct of unexampled absurdity? What bar-riers have you to oppose to this most strong energetic Govern-ment? To that Government you have nothing to oppose. All your defence is given up. This is a real actual defect.—It must strike the mind of every Gentleman. When our Government was first insti-tuted in Virginia, we declared the common law of England to be in force.—That system of law which has been admired, and has protected us and our ancestors, is excluded by that system.— Added to this, we adopted a Bill of Rights. By this Constitution, some of the best barriers of human rights are thrown away. Is there not an additional reason to have a Bill of Rights? By the an-cient common law, the trial of all facts is decided by a jury of im-partial men from the immediate vicinage. This paper speaks of different juries from the common law, in criminal cases; and in civil controversies excludes trial by jury altogether. There is there-fore more occasion for the supplementary check of a Bill of Rights now, than then. Congress from their general powers may fully go into the business of human legislation. They may legislate in crim-inal cases from treason to the lowest offence, petty larceny. They may define crimes and prescribe punishments. In the definition of crimes, I trust they will be directed by what wise Representa-tives ought to be governed by. But when we come to punishments, no latitude ought to be left, nor dependence put on the virtue of Representatives. What says our Bill of Rights? "That excessive bail ought not to be required, nor excessive fines imposed, nor cruel and unusual punishments inflicted." Are you not therefore now calling on those Gentlemen who are to compose Congress, to pre-scribe trials and define punishments without this controul? Will they find sentiments there similar to this Bill of Rights? You let them loose—you do more—you depart from the genius of your country. That paper tells you, that the trial of crimes shall be by jury, and held in the State where the crime shall have been committed.—Under this extensive provision, they may proceed in a manner extremely dangerous to liberty.—Persons accused may be carried from one extremity of the State to another, and be tried not by an impartial jury of the vicinage, acquainted with his character, and the circumstances of the fact; but by a jury unacquainted with both, and who may be biassed against him.—Is not this sufficient to alarm men?—How different is this from the immemorial practice of your British ancestors, and your own? I need not tell you, that by the [English] common law a number of hundredors [residents from the same group of one hundred] were required to be on a jury, and that afterwards it was sufficient if the jurors came from the same county. With less than this the people of England have never been satisfied. That paper ought to have declared the common law in force.

The Rights of Human Nature

In this business of legislation, your Members of Congress will lose the restriction of not imposing excessive fines, demanding excessive bail, and inflicting cruel and unusual punishments.—These are prohibited by your Declaration of Rights. What has distinguished our ancestors?—That they would not admit of tortures, or cruel and barbarous punishments. But Congress may introduce the practice of the civil law, in preference to that of the common law.—They may introduce the practice of France, Spain, and Germany—Of torturing to extort a confession of the crime. They will say that they might as well draw examples from those countries as from Great-Britain; and they will tell you, that there is such a necessity of strengthening the arm of Government that they must have a criminal equity, and extort confession by torture, in order to punish with still more relentless severity. We are then lost and undone.—And can any man think it troublesome, when we can by a small interference prevent our rights from being lost?—If you will, like the Virginian Government, give them knowledge of the extent of the rights retained by the people, and the powers themselves, they will, if they be honest men, thank you for it.—Will they not wish to go on sure grounds?—But if you leave them otherwise, they will not know how to proceed; and being in a state of uncertainty, they will assume rather than give up powers by implication. A Bill of Rights may be summed up in a few words.

Patrick Henry argued that the Constitution must have a Bill of Rights in order to protect the freedoms of the American people.

What do they tell us?—That our rights are reserved.—Why not say so? Is it because it will consume too much paper? Gentlemen's reasonings against a Bill of Rights, do not satisfy me. Without saying which has the right side, it remains doubtful. A Bill of Rights is a favourite thing with the Virginians, and the people of the other States likewise. It may be their prejudice, but the Government ought to suit their geniuses, otherwise its operation will be unhappy. A Bill of Rights, even if its necessity be doubtful, will exclude the possibility of dispute, and with great submission, I think the best way is to have no dispute. In the present Constitution, they are restrained from issuing general warrants to search suspected places, or seize persons not named, without evidence of the commission of the fact, &c. There was certainly some celestial influence governing those who deliberated on that Constitution:— For they have with the most cautious and enlightened circumspection, guarded those indefeasible rights, which ought ever to be held sacred. The officers of Congress may come upon you, fortified with all the terrors of paramount federal authority.—Excisemen may come in multitudes:—For the limitation of their numbers no man knows.—They may, unless the General Government be restrained by a Bill of Rights, or some similar restriction, go into your cellars and rooms, and search, ransack and measure, every thing you eat, drink and wear. They ought to be restrained within proper bounds. With respect to the freedom of the press, I need say nothing; for it is hoped that the Gentlemen who shall compose Congress, will take care as little as possible, to infringe the rights of human nature.—This will result from their integrity. They should from prudence, abstain from violating the rights of their constituents. They are not however expressly restrained.—But whether they will intermeddle with that palladium of our liberties or not, I leave you to determine.

17 June 1788

[Editor's note: In the following argument Henry examines the ninth section of Article I of the Constitution and argues that it is a meager substitute for a substantive bill of rights.]

Mr. Chairman.—We have now come to the ninth section [of Article I], and I consider myself at liberty to take a short view of the whole. I wish to do it very briefly. Give me leave to remark, that there is a Bill of Rights in that Government [established by the Constitution]. There are express restrictions which are in the shape of a Bill of Rights: But they bear the name of the ninth section. The design of the negative expressions in this section is to prescribe limits, beyond which the powers of Congress shall not go. These are the sole bounds intended by the American Government. Where abouts do we stand with respect to a Bill of Rights? Examine it, and compare it to the idea manifested by the Virginian Bill of Rights, or that of the other States. The restraints in this Congressional Bill of Rights, are so feeble and few, that it would have been infinitely better to have said nothing about it. The fair implication is, that they can do every thing they are not forbidden to do. What will be the result if Congress, in the course of their legislation, should do a thing not restrained by this ninth section? It will fall as an incidental power to Congress, not being prohibited expressly in the Constitution. The first prohibition is, that the privilege of the writ of *habeas corpus* shall not be suspended, but when in cases of rebellion, or invasion, the public safety may require it. It results clearly, that if it had not said so, they could suspend it in all cases whatsoever. It reverses the position of the friends of this Constitution, that every thing is retained which is not given up. For instead of this, every thing is given up, which is not expressly reserved. . . .

You are told, that your rights are secured in this new Government. They are guarded in no other part but this ninth section. The few restrictions in that section are your only safeguards. They may controul your actions, and your very words, without being repugnant to that paper. The existence of your dearest privileges will depend on the consent of Congress: For these are not within the restrictions of the ninth section.

If Gentlemen think that securing the slave trade is a capital object; that the privilege of the *habeas corpus* is sufficiently secured; that the exclusion of *ex post facto* laws will produce no inconvenience; that the publication from time to time will secure their property; in one word, that this section alone will sufficiently secure their liberties, I have spoken in vain.—Every word of mine, and of my worthy coadjutor [George Mason], is lost. I trust that Gentlemen, on this occasion, will see the great objects of religion, liberty of the press, trial by jury, interdiction of cruel punishments, and every other sacred right secured, before they agree to that paper. These most important human rights are not protected by that section, which is the only safeguard in the Constitution.—My mind will not be quieted till I see something substantial come forth in the shape of a Bill of Rights.

Viewpoint 6

"I conceive every fair reasoner will agree, that there is no just cause to suspect that they [rights] will be violated."

The Constitution Does Not Need a Bill of Rights

Edmund Randolph

Edmund Randolph, who served as governor of Virginia from 1786 to 1788, began as an Anti-Federalist (he even refused to sign the Constitution at first) but eventually became a supporter of the new Constitution. The words that follow are his direct response to Patrick Henry's June 17, 1788, speech calling for a bill of rights. Randolph made the case that, as written, the Constitution contained no provisions that appeared to threaten people's civil rights; furthermore, he said, the system of checks and balances set forth in the document seemed sufficient to safeguard the people from tyranny.

I declared some days ago that I would give my suffrage for this Constitution, not because I considered it without blemish, but because the critical situation of our country demanded it. I invite

David Robertson, ed., *Debates and Other Proceedings of the Convention of Virginia.* Richmond, VA: Inquirer Press, 1805.

those who think with me to vote for the Constitution.—But where things occur in it which I disapprove of, I shall be candid in exposing my objections. . . .

On the subject of a Bill of Rights, the want of which has been complained of, I will observe that it has been sanctified by such reverend authority, that I feel some difficulty in going against it. I shall not, however, be deterred from giving my opinion on this occasion, let the consequence be what it may. At the beginning of the [Revolutionary] war we had no certain Bill of Rights: For our charter cannot be considered as a Bill of Rights. It is nothing more than an investiture in the hands of the Virginian citizens, of those rights which belonged to the British subjects. When the British thought proper to infringe our rights, was it not necessary to mention in our Constitution, those rights which ought to be paramount to the power of the Legislature? Why are the Bill of Rights distinct from the Constitution? I consider Bills of Rights in this view, that the Government should use them when there is a departure from its fundamental principles, in order to restore them. This is the true sense of a Bill of Rights. If it be consistent with the Constitution, or contains additional rights, why not put it in the Constitution? If it be repugnant to the Constitution, there will be a perpetual scene of warfare between them. The Honorable Gentleman [Patrick Henry] has praised the Bill of Rights of Virginia, and called it his guardian angel, and vilified this Constitution for not having it. Give me leave to make a distinction between the Representatives of the people of a particular country, who are appointed as the ordinary Legislature, having no limitation to their powers, and another body arising from a compact and certain delineated powers. Were a Bill of Rights necessary in the former, it would not in the latter; for the best security that can be in the latter is the express enumeration of its powers. But let me ask the Gentleman where his favourite rights are violated? They are not violated by the tenth section, which contains restrictions on the States. Are they violated by the enumerated powers? . . . —Is there not provision made in this Constitution for the trial by jury in criminal cases? Does not the third article provide, that the trial of all crimes shall be by jury, and held in the State where the said crimes shall have been committed? Does it not follow, that the cause and nature of the accusation must be produced, because otherwise they cannot proceed on the cause? Every one knows, that the witnesses must be brought before the jury, or else the prisoner will be discharged. Calling for evidence in his favor is co-incident to his trial. There is no suspicion, that less than twelve jurors will be thought sufficient. The only defect is, that there is no speedy trial.—Consider how this could have been amended. We have heard complaints against it, because it is supposed the jury is to come from the State at large. It will be in their power to have juries from the vicinage. And would not the complaints have been louder, if they had appointed a Federal Court to be had in every county in the State?—Criminals are brought in this State from every part of the country to the General Court, and jurors from the vicinage are summoned to the trials. There can be no reason to prevent the General Government from adopting a similar regulation.

A Constitution for Thirteen States, Not One

As to the exclusion of excessive bail and fines, and cruel and unusual punishments, this would follow of itself without a Bill of Rights. Observations have been made about watchfulness over those in power, which deserve our attention. There must be a combination—We must presume corruption in the House of Representatives, Senate, and President, before we can suppose that excessive fines can be imposed, or cruel punishments inflicted. Their number is the highest security.—Numbers are the highest security in our own Constitution, which has attracted so many eulogiums from the Gentleman. Here we have launched into a sea of suspicions. How shall we check power?—By their numbers. Before these cruel punishments can be inflicted, laws must be passed, and Judges must judge contrary to justice. This would excite universal discontent, and detestation of the Members of the Government. They might involve their friends in the calamities resulting from it, and could be removed from office. I never desire a greater security than this, which I believe to be absolutely sufficient.

That general warrants are grievous and oppressive, and ought not to be granted, I fully admit. I heartily concur in expressing my detestation of them. But we have sufficient security here also. We do not rely on the integrity of any one particular person or body;

but on the number and different orders of the Members of the Government: Some of them having necessarily the same feelings with ourselves. Can it be believed, that the Federal Judiciary would not be independent enough to prevent such oppressive practices? If they will not do justice to persons injured, may they not go to our own State Judiciaries and obtain it?

Gentlemen have been misled to a certain degree, by a general declaration, that the trial by jury was gone. We see that in the most valuable cases, it is reserved. Is it abolished in civil cases? Let him put his finger on the part where it is abolished. The Constitution is silent on it.—What expression would you wish the constitution to use, to establish it? Remember we were not making a Constitution for Virginia alone, or we might have taken Virginia for our directory. But we were forming a Constitution for thirteen States. The trial by jury is different in different States. In some States it is excluded in cases in which it is admitted in others. In Admiralty causes it is not used. Would you have a jury to determine the case of a capture? The Virginian Legislature thought proper to make an exception of that case. These depend on the law of nations, and no twelve men that could be picked up would be equal to the decision of such a matter.

We Must Avoid Anarchy

Then, Sir, the freedom of the press is said to be insecure. God forbid that I should give my voice against the freedom of the press. But I ask, (and with confidence that it cannot be answered) where is the page where it is restrained? If there had been any regulation about it, leaving it insecure, then there might have been reason for clamours. But this is not the case. If it be, I again ask for the particular clause which gives liberty to destroy the freedom of the press.

He has added religion to the objects endangered in his conception. Is there any power given over it? Let it be pointed out. Will he not be contented with the answer which has been frequently given to that objection? That variety of sects which abounds in the United States is the best security for the freedom of religion. No part of the Constitution, even if strictly construed, will justify a conclusion, that the General Government can take away, or impair the freedom of religion.

The Gentleman asks with triumph, shall we be deprived of these valuable rights? Had there been an exception, or express infringement of those rights, he might object.—But I conceive every fair reasoner will agree, that there is no just cause to suspect that they will be violated.

But he objects, that the common law is not established by the Constitution. The wisdom of the Convention is displayed by its omission; because the common law ought not to be immutably fixed. Is it established in our own Constitution, or the Bill of Rights which has been resounded through the House? It is established only by an act of the Legislature, and can therefore be changed as circumstances may require it. Let the Honorable Gentleman consider what would be the destructive consequences of its establishment in the Constitution. Even in England, where the firmest opposition has been made to encroachments upon it, it has been frequently changed. What would have been our dilemma if it had been established?—Virginia has declared, that children shall have equal portions of the real estates of their intestate parents, and it is consistent to the principles of a Republican Government.—The immutable establishment of the common law, would have been repugnant to that regulation. It would in many respects be destructive to republican principles, and productive of great inconveniences. I might indulge myself, by shewing many parts of the common law which would have this effect. I hope I shall not be thought to speak ludicrously, when I say, that the *writ* of *burning heretics*, would have been revived by it. It would tend to throw real property in few hands, and prevent the introduction of many salutary regulations. Thus, were the common law adopted in that system, it would destroy the principles of Republican Government. But it is not excluded. It may be established by an act of the Legislature. Its defective parts may be altered, and it may be changed and modified as the convenience of the public may require it. . . .

I cast my eyes to the actual situation of America; I see the dreadful tempest, to which the present calm is a prelude, if disunion takes place. I see the anarchy which must happen if no energetic Government be established. In this situation, I would take the Constitution were it more objectionable than it is.—For if anarchy and confusion follow disunion, an enterprising man may enter into the American throne. I conceive there is no danger. The Representatives are chosen by and from among the people. They will have a fellow-feeling for the farmers and planters. The twenty-six Senators, Representatives of the States, will not be those desperadoes and horrid adventurers which they are represented to be. The State Legislatures, I trust, will not forget the duty they owe to their country so far, as to choose such men to manage their federal interests. I trust, that the Members of Congress themselves, will explain the ambiguous parts: And if not, the States can combine in order to insist on amending the ambiguities. I would depend on the present actual feelings of the people of America, to introduce any amendment which may be necessary. I repeat it again, though I do not reverence the Constitution, that its adoption is necessary to avoid the storm which is hanging over America, and that no greater curse can befal her, than the dissolution of the political connection between the States. Whether we shall propose previous or subsequent amendments, is now the only dispute. It is supererogation to repeat again the arguments in support of each.—But I ask Gentlemen, whether, as eight States have adopted it, it be not safer to adopt it, and rely on the probability of obtaining amendments, than by a rejection to hazard a breach of the Union?

CHAPTER 3

The Question of Slavery

✸ Chapter Preface

The debate among the Constitution's framers about slavery and whether or not the slave trade, or perhaps slavery itself, should be banned was not new to American political discussion. A number of the founding fathers, including John Adams and Thomas Jefferson, had long had certain moral or other reservations about slavery. In fact, Jefferson himself had earlier tried to eliminate, or at least take a stand against, the institution in two key political documents he had penned.

The first instance was a brief statement in the list of grievances in the preamble to Virginia's state constitution. In Jefferson's words, the British king had, "through the inhuman use of his negative . . . refused us permission to exclude [slavery] by law." This implied that the American patriots had always desired to end the slave trade but had been stopped from doing so by British law. In truth, though, most of the southern colonies had always been and still were eager participants in the slave trade because it was a cornerstone of their economies. Thus, blaming the British for the slave trade was partly designed to make it look to the world as if the Americans, who talked incessantly about human liberty, were not really responsible for the evils of slavery.

Jefferson tackled the slavery issue in a much more substantial and controversial manner in his rough draft for the Declaration of Independence, composed in June 1776. To make this moral stand against the slave trade as strong as possible, he significantly lengthened the short statement he had included in the Virginia document. The slave trade, the new version read in part, amounted to a

> cruel war against human nature itself, violating its most sacred rights of life and liberty in the persons of a distant people [i.e., black Africans] . . . captivating and carrying them into slavery in another hemisphere, or to incur miserable death in their transportation thither [from there to here].

The passage went on to call the slave trade "piratical warfare," "execrable [repulsive] commerce," an "assemblage of horrors," a crime "committed against the liberties of one people," and murder.

Needless to say, this totally unexpected, vehement, and emotional assault on the slave trade did not sit well with the congressional delegates from several of the southern colonies (soon to be states). Many of these men could agree with Jefferson in principle that slavery was ultimately wrong. But they were not about to give up either the slave trade or their slaves. So Jefferson's attack on slavery was summarily excised from the Declaration of Independence. The issue came up again when the same men were writing the Constitution; and once more, entrenched economic interests won out over ethical concerns. Despite their considerable political wisdom, the founders did not foresee that it would take a bloody civil war to resolve the issue of slavery in the United States.

Viewpoint 1

"The Society implore[s] the present Convention to make the Suppression of the African trade in the United States, a part of their important deliberations."

The Constitution Should Ban the Slave Trade

Pennsylvania Society for the Abolition of Slavery

The Pennsylvania Society for the Abolition of Slavery, created in 1775, was the first abolitionist organization in the United States. In 1787 members of the group drew up a petition calling for the delegates to the Constitutional Convention to prohibit the slave trade. The society then handed the petition, reproduced here, to Pennsylvania delegate Benjamin Franklin to submit to the Convention in a formal manner. However, Franklin did not submit it, fearing that it would stir up too much anger among the delegates from the southern states, who insisted that they would not even consider signing a Constitution that outlawed slavery. Nevertheless, some of the same arguments outlined in the petition were voiced by other concerned delegates during the constitutional debates.

Pennsylvania Society for the Abolition of Slavery, petition to the Constitutional Convention, June 2, 1787.

To the honorable the Convention of the United States of America now assembled in the City of Philadelphia. The memorial of the Pennsylvania Society for promoting the Abolition of Slavery and the relief of free Negroes unlawfully held in bondage.

The Pennsylvania Society for promoting the Abolition of Slavery and the relief of free Negroes unlawfully held in Bondage rejoice with their fellow Citizens in beholding a Convention of the States assembled for the purpose of amending the federal Constitution.

They recollect with pleasure, that among the first Acts of the illustrious [Continental] Congress of the Year 1774 was a resolution for prohibiting the Importation of African Slaves.

It is with deep distress they are forced to observe that the peace was scarcely concluded before the African Trade was revived and American Vessels employed in transporting the Inhabitants of Africa to cultivate as Slaves the soil of America before it had drank in all the blood which had been shed in her struggle for liberty.

To the revival of this trade the Society ascribe part of the Obloquy with which foreign Nations have branded our infant States. In vain will be their Pretentions to a love of liberty or a regard for national Character, while they share in the profits of a Commerce that can only be conducted upon Rivers of human tears and Blood.

By all the Attributes, therefore, of the Deity which are offended by this inhuman traffic—by the Union of our whole species in a common Ancestor and by all the Obligations which result from it—by the apprehensions and terror of the righteous Vengeance of God in national Judgements—by the certainty of the great and awful day of retribution—by the efficacy of the Prayers of good Men, which would only insult the Majesty of Heaven, if offered up in behalf of our Country while the Iniquity we deplore continues among us—by the sanctity of the Christian Name—by the Pleasures of domestic Connections and the pangs which attend their Dissolutions—by the Captivity and Sufferings of our *American* bretheren in Algiers which seem to be intended by divine Providence to awaken us to a Sense of the Injustice and Cruelty of dooming our *African* Bretheren to perpetual Slavery and Misery—by a regard to the consistency of principles and Conduct which should mark the Citizens of Republics—by the magnitude and intensity of our desires to promote the happiness of those millions of intelligent beings who will probably cover this immense Continent with rational life—and by every other consideration that religion Reason Policy and Humanity can suggest the Society implore the present Convention to make the Suppression of the African trade in the United States, a part of their important deliberations.

                          Signed by order of the Society

June the 2 1787

                          Jonathan Penrose Vice President

Viewpoint 2

"By this article after the year 1808, the congress will have power to prohibit such importation. . . . I consider this as laying the foundation for banishing slavery."

It Is Necessary to Retain the Slave Trade

James Wilson

Many of the delegates to the Constitutional Convention agreed with the sentiments expressed by the Pennsylvania Society for the Abolition of Slavery. Although slavery was still legal and widely accepted by many people, increasing numbers of Americans felt that the institution contradicted the lofty principles of freedom and human dignity expressed in the Declaration of Independence and the new Constitution itself. Thomas Jefferson and James Madison, both of them slave owners, felt this way, as did men like Pennsylvania's James Wilson, one of the leading framers of the Constitution. However, it was clear to these men that the southern states would not agree to any constitutional provision that banned the slave trade. So some kind of compromise that allowed the trade to go on at least in the short run was needed. As Madison put it in a speech delivered in Virginia in

Thomas Lloyd, ed., *Debates of the Convention of the State of Pennsylvania on the Constitution, Proposed for the Government of the United States.* Philadelphia, 1788.

June 1788: "The southern states would not have entered into the Union of America without the temporary permission of the trade. And if they were excluded from the Union, the consequences might be dreadful to them and to us. . . . Great as the evil is, a dismemberment of the Union would be worse. If those states should disunite from the other states, for not indulging them in the temporary continuance of this traffic, they might solicit and obtain aid from foreign powers." Wilson agreed that a compromise was necessary and said so in the following statement he made on December 3, 1787, in his home state. By putting off possible prohibition of the slave trade for some two decades, he argued, the Union would remain intact, while the odious traffic in slaves would gradually be extinguished.

W ith respect to the clause, restricting congress from prohibiting the migration or importation of such persons, as any of the states now existing, shall think proper to admit, prior to the year 1808. The honorable gentleman [William Findley] says, that this clause is not only dark, but intended to grant to congress, for that time, the power to admit the importation of slaves. No such thing was intended; but I will tell you what was done, and it give me high pleasure, that so much was done. Under the present confederation, the states may admit the importation of slaves as long as they please; but by this article after the year 1808, the congress will have power to prohibit such importation, notwithstanding the disposition of any state to the contrary. I consider this as laying the foundation for banishing slavery out of this country; and though the period is more distant than I could wish, yet it will produce the same kind, gradual change, which was pursued in Pennsylvania. It is with much satisfaction I view this power in the general government, whereby they may lay an interdiction on this reproachful trade; but an immediate advantage is also obtained, for a tax or duty may be imposed on such importation, not exceeding ten dollars for each person; and, this sir, operates as a partial prohibition; it was all that could be obtained, I am sorry it was no more; but from this I think there is reason to hope, that yet a few years, and it will be prohibited altogether; and in the mean time, the new states which are to be formed, will be under the control of congress in this particular; and slaves will never be introduced amongst them.

The gentleman says, that it is unfortunate in another point of view; it means to prohibit the introduction of white people from Europe, as this tax may deter them from coming amongst us; a little impartiality and attention will discover the care that the convention took in selecting their language. The words are, the *migration or* IMPORTATION of such persons, &c. shall not be prohibited by congress prior to the year 1808, but a tax or duty may be imposed on such IMPORTATION; it is observable here, that the term migration is dropped, when a tax or duty is mentioned; so that congress have power to impose the tax, only on those imported.

Viewpoint 3

"Slavery was an evil to be tolerated, allowed to enter the Constitution only by the back door."

The Framers Who Opposed Slavery Had No Other Choice but Compromise

Herbert J. Storing

The surviving statements of James Wilson, James Madison, Thomas Jefferson, and other early American leaders who opposed the slave trade demonstrate that they felt they had no other choice but to compromise with the southerners who demanded the trade remain intact. But seen in retrospect, was the issue really so divisive that compromise was the only option? One modern historian who feels it was is Herbert J. Storing, author of the well-reviewed *What the Anti-Federalists Were For* and other books about the Anti-Federalists. In the following essay, Storing expresses regret that the slaves were condemned to continue their suffering in order that the Union should not be torn asunder. But he suggests that the compromise the anti-slavery framers made did not imply that they approved of slavery on moral grounds.

Herbert J. Storing, "Slavery and the Moral Foundations of the American Republic," *The Moral Foundations of the American Republic*, edited by Robert H. Horwitz. Charlottesville: University Press of Virginia, 1986. Copyright © 1986 by Kenyon Public Affairs Conference Center. Reproduced by permission of the publisher.

The Founders did acknowledge slavery; they compromised with it. The effect was in the short run probably to strengthen it. Perhaps they could have done more to restrict it, though the words of a Missouri judge express what the Founders thought they were doing and, I think, probably the truth. "When the States assumed the rights of self-government, they found their citizens claiming a right of property in a miserable portion of the human race. Sound national policy required that the evil should be restricted as much as possible. What they could, they did." "As those fathers marked it," [Abraham] Lincoln urged on the eve of the Civil War, "so let it be again marked, as an evil not to be extended, but to be tolerated and protected only because of and so far as its actual presence among us makes that toleration and protection a necessity." Slavery was an evil to be tolerated, allowed to enter the Constitution only by the back door, grudgingly, unacknowledged, on the presumption that the house would be truly fit to live in only when it was gone, and that it would ultimately be gone.

In their accommodation to slavery, the Founders limited and confined it and carefully withheld any indication of moral approval, while they built a Union that they thought was the greatest instrument of human liberty ever made, that they thought would lead and that did in fact lead to the extinction of Negro slavery. It is common today to make harsh reference to the irony of ringing declarations of human rights coming from the pens of men who owned slaves. . . . They saw better than their critics how difficult it was to extricate themselves from that [ironic] position in a reasonably equitable way. But they saw, too, a deeper irony: these masters knew that they were writing the texts in which their slaves would learn their rights.

Pursuing Happiness as One Sees Fit

Having, I hope, rescued the Founders from the common charge that they shamefully excluded Negroes from the principles of the Declaration of Independence, that they regarded their enslavement as just, and that in their Constitution they protected property in man like any other property, I must at least touch on a deeper question, where they do not come off so well. But at this deeper level the problem is not that they betrayed their principles, the common charge; the problem lies rather in the principles themselves. That very principle of individual liberty for which the Founders worked so brilliantly and successfully contains within itself an uncomfortably large opening toward slavery. The principle is the right of each individual to his life, his liberty, his pursuit of happiness as he sees fit. He is, to be sure, subject to constraints in the pursuit of his own interests because of the fact of other human beings with similar rights. But are these moral constraints or merely prudential ones? [English philosopher John] Locke says that under the law of nature each individual ought, as much as he can, "to preserve the rest of mankind" "when his own preservation comes not in competition." Each individual is of course the judge of what his own preservation does require, and it would be a foolish man, an unnatural man, who would not, under conditions of extreme uncertainty, give himself every generous benefit of the doubt. Does this not tend to mean in practice that each individual has a right to pursue his own interests, as he sees fit and as he can? And is there not a strong tendency for that "as he can" to become conclusive? In civil society, indeed, each of us gives up the claim of sovereign judgment for the sake of the milder, surer benefits of a supreme judge. Even in that case there is a question whether the first principle does not remain that one may do what one can do. The Founders often described the problem of civil society as resulting from that tendency. In any case, regarding persons outside civil society, there is a strong implication that any duty I have to respect their rights is whatever residue is left after I have amply secured my own.

"A Wolf by the Ears"

Now, in the case of American slavery, especially in the South at the time of the writing of the Constitution, there clearly was a conflict between the rights of the slaves and the self-preservation of the masters. "[W]e have a wolf by the ears," Jefferson said, "and we can neither hold him, nor safely let him go. Justice is in one scale, and self preservation in the other." Only an invincible naiveté can deny that Jefferson spoke truly. But the deeper issue, as I think Jefferson knew, is the tendency, under the principles of the Declaration of Independence itself, for justice to be reduced to self-preservation, for self-preservation to be defined as self-interest, and for self-interest to be defined as what is convenient and achievable. Thus the slave owner may resolve that it is necessary to keep his slaves in bondage for the compelling reason that if they were free they would kill him; but he may also decide, on the same basic principle, that he must keep them enslaved in order to protect his plantation, his children's patrimony, his flexibility of action, on which his preservation ultimately depends; and from that he may conclude that he is entitled to keep his slaves in bondage if he finds it convenient to do so. All of this presumes of course that he *can* keep his slaves in bondage. Nor does it in any way deny the right of the slave to resist his enslavement and to act the part of the master if he can. This whole chain of reasoning is a chilling clarification of the essential war that seems always to exist, at bottom, between man and man.

American Negro slavery, in this ironic and terrible sense, can be seen as a radicalization of the principle of individual liberty on which the American polity was founded. Jefferson wrote in his *Notes on the State of Virginia* of the demoralization of the masters caused by slavery and its threat to the whole institution of free government. Masters become tyrants and teach tyranny to their children (and, incidentally, to their slaves). Even more important, slavery, through its visible injustice, tends to destroy the moral foundation of civil society. "And can the liberties of a nation be thought secure when we have removed their only firm basis, a conviction in the minds of the people that these liberties are of the gift of God? That they are not to be violated but with His wrath? Indeed I tremble for my country when I reflect that God is just; that his justice cannot sleep forever; that . . . an exchange of situation [between whites and blacks] is among possible events; that it may become probably [*sic*] by supernatural interference! The Almighty has no attribute which can take side with us in such a contest." I do not think that Jefferson was literally concerned with divine vengeance, but he was concerned with the underlying tension—so ruthlessly exposed in the institution of Negro slavery—between the doctrine of individual rights and the necessary moral ground of any government instituted to secure those rights.

Viewpoint 4

"The effects of the framers' compromise have remained for generations. They arose from the contradiction between guaranteeing liberty and justice to all, and denying both to Negroes."

The Framers Who Opposed Slavery Should Not Have Compromised on the Issue

Thurgood Marshall

Thurgood Marshall was the first African American to serve on the U.S. Supreme Court, a post he held with distinction from 1967 to 1991. In the following speech, which he gave on May 6, 1987, to the annual seminar of the San Francisco Patent and Trademark Law Association in anticipation of the coming celebrations of the bicentennial of the U.S. Constitution, he was critical of the framers for what he saw as major defects in the original document. In particular, he focused on the failure of the founders to eradicate the slave trade. Doing so, Marshall, contended, would have conformed to the spirit of equality expressed repeatedly in the Constitution and Declaration of Independence. Instead, the founders—even those who claimed to feel slavery was wrong—compromised their own principles and created a legal framework that allowed several more generations of African Americans to suffer needlessly. Clearly, Marshall felt that the framers who opposed slavery should have stood up for their principles and created a constitution that did not require a civil war and numerous amendments to make it the great document it is today.

The year 1987 marks the 200th anniversary of the United States Constitution. A Commission has been established to coordinate the celebration. The official meetings, essay contests, and festivities have begun.

The planned commemoration will span three years, and I am told 1987 is 'dedicated to the memory of the Founders and the document they drafted in Philadelphia.' We are to 'recall the achievements of our Founders and the knowledge and experience that inspired them, the nature of the government they established, its origins, its character, and its ends, and the rights and privileges of citizenship, as well as its attendant responsibilities.'

Like many anniversary celebrations, the plan for 1987 takes particular events and holds them up as the source of all the very best that has followed. Patriotic feelings will surely swell, prompting proud proclamations of the wisdom, foresight, and sense of justice shared by the framers and reflected in a written document now yellowed with age. This is unfortunate—not the patriotism itself, but the tendency for the celebration to oversimplify, and overlook the many other events that have been instrumental to our achievements as a nation. The focus of this celebration invites a complacent belief that the vision of those who debated and compromised in Philadelphia yielded the 'more perfect Union' it is said we now enjoy.

I cannot accept this invitation, for I do not believe that the meaning of the Constitution was forever 'fixed' at the Philadelphia Convention. Nor do I find the wisdom, foresight, and sense of justice exhibited by the framers particularly profound. To the contrary, the government they devised was defective from the start, requiring several amendments, a civil war, and momentous social transformation to attain the system of constitutional government, and its respect for the individual freedoms and human rights, that we hold as fundamental today. When contemporary Americans cite 'The Constitution,' they invoke a concept that is vastly different from what the framers barely began to construct two centuries ago.

Moral Principles Compromised

For a sense of the evolving nature of the Constitution we need look no further than the first three words of the document's preamble: 'We the People.' When the Founding Fathers used this phrase in 1787, they did not have in mind the majority of America's citizens. 'We the People' included, in the words of the framers, 'the whole Number of free Persons.' On a matter so basic as the right to vote, for example, Negro slaves were excluded, although they were counted for representational purposes—at three-fifths each. Women did not gain the right to vote for over a hundred and thirty years.

These omissions were intentional. The record of the framers' debates on the slave question is especially clear: the Southern states acceded to the demands of the New England states for giving Congress broad power to regulate commerce, in exchange for the right to continue the slave trade. The economic interests of the regions coalesced: New Englanders engaged in the 'carrying trade' would profit from transporting slaves from Africa as well as goods produced in America by slave labor. The perpetuation of slavery ensured the primary source of wealth in the Southern states.

Despite this clear understanding of the role slavery would play in the new republic, use of the words 'slaves' and 'slavery' was carefully avoided in the original document. Political representation in the lower House of Congress was to be based on the population of 'free Persons' in each state, plus three-fifths of all 'other Persons.' Moral principles against slavery, for those who had them, were compromised, with no explanation of the conflicting principles for which the American Revolutionary War had ostensibly been fought: the self-evident truths 'that all men are created equal, that they are endowed by their Creator with certain unalienable Rights, that among these are Life, Liberty and the pursuit of Happiness.'

It was not the first such compromise. Even these ringing phrases from the Declaration of Independence are filled with irony, for an early draft of what became that declaration assailed the King of England for suppressing legislative attempts to end the slave trade and for encouraging slave rebellions. The final draft adopted in 1776 did not contain this criticism. And so again at the Constitutional Convention eloquent objections to the institution of slavery went unheeded, and its opponents eventually consented to a document which laid a foundation for the tragic events that were to follow.

"Beings of an Inferior Order"

Pennsylvania's Gouverneur Morris provides an example. He opposed slavery and the counting of slaves in determining the basis for representation in Congress. At the Convention he objected that the inhabitant of Georgia [or] South Carolina who goes to the coast of Africa, and in defiance of the most sacred laws of humanity tears away his fellow creatures from their dearest connections and damns them to the most cruel bondages, shall have more votes in a Government instituted for protection of the rights of mankind, than the Citizen of Pennsylvania or New Jersey who views with a laudable horror, so nefarious a practice.

And yet Gouverneur Morris eventually accepted the three-fifths accommodation. In fact, he wrote the final draft of the Constitution, the very document the bicentennial will commemorate.

As a result of compromise, the right of the Southern states to continue importing slaves was extended, officially, at least until 1808. We know that it actually lasted a good deal longer, as the framers possessed no monopoly on the ability to trade moral principles for self-interest. But they nevertheless set an unfortunate example. Slaves could be imported, if the commercial interests of the North were protected. To make the compromise even more palatable, customs duties would be imposed at up to ten dollars per slave as a means of raising public revenues.

No doubt it will be said, when the unpleasant truth of the his-

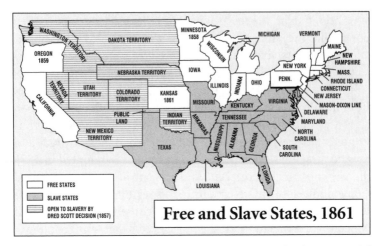

Free and Slave States, 1861

tory of slavery in America is mentioned during this bicentennial year, that the Constitution was a product of its times, and embodied a compromise which, under other circumstances, would not have been made. But the effects of the framers' compromise have remained for generations. They arose from the contradiction between guaranteeing liberty and justice to all, and denying both to Negroes.

The original intent of the phrase, 'We the People,' was far too clear for any ameliorating construction. Writing for the Supreme Court in 1857, Chief Justice Taney penned the following passage in the Dred Scott case, on the issue of whether, in the eyes of the framers, slaves were 'constituent members of the sovereignty,' and were to be included among 'We the People':

> We think they are not, and that they are not included, and were not intended to be included . . . .
>
> . . . . They had for more than a century before been regarded as beings of an inferior order, and altogether unfit to associate with the white race . . . ; and so far inferior, that they had no rights which the white man was bound to respect; and that the negro might justly and lawfully be reduced to slavery for his benefit. . . .
>
> . . . [A]ccordingly, a negro of the African race was regarded . . . as an article of property, and held, and bought and sold as

such. . . . [N]o one seems to have doubted the correctness of the prevailing opinion of the time.

"Promises Not Fulfilled"

And so, nearly seven decades after the Constitutional Convention, the Supreme Court reaffirmed the prevailing opinion of the framers regarding the rights of Negroes in America. It took a bloody civil war before the thirteenth amendment could be adopted to abolish slavery, though not the consequences slavery would have for future Americans.

While the Union survived the civil war, the Constitution did not. In its place arose a new, more promising basis for justice and equality, the fourteenth amendment, ensuring protection of the life, liberty, and property of all persons against deprivations without due process, and guaranteeing equal protection of the laws. And yet almost another century would pass before any significant recognition was obtained of the rights of black Americans to share equally even in such basic opportunities as education, housing, and employment, and to have their votes counted, and counted equally. In the meantime, blacks joined America's military to fight its wars and invested untold hours working in its factories and on its farms, contributing to the development of this country's magnificent wealth and waiting to share in its prosperity.

What is striking is the role legal principles have played throughout America's history in determining the condition of Negroes. They were enslaved by law, emancipated by law, disenfranchised and segregated by law; and, finally, they have begun to win equality by law. Along the way, new constitutional principles have emerged to meet the challenges of a changing society. The progress has been dramatic, and it will continue.

The men who gathered in Philadelphia in 1787 could not have envisioned these changes. They could not have imagined, nor would they have accepted, that the document they were drafting would one day be construed by a Supreme Court to which had been appointed a woman and the descendent of an African slave. 'We the People' no longer enslave, but the credit does not belong to the framers. It belongs to those who refused to acquiesce in outdated notions of 'liberty,' 'justice,' and 'equality,' and who strived to better them.

And so we must be careful, when focusing on the events which took place in Philadelphia two centuries ago, that we not overlook the momentous events which followed, and thereby lose our proper sense of perspective. Otherwise, the odds are that for many Americans the bicentennial celebration will be little more than a blind pilgrimage to the shrine of the original document now stored in a vault in the National Archives. If we seek, instead, a sensitive understanding of the Constitution's inherent defects, and its promising evolution through 200 years of history, the celebration of the 'Miracle at Philadelphia' will, in my view, be a far more meaningful and humbling experience. We will see that the true miracle was not the birth of the Constitution, but its life, a life nurtured through two turbulent centuries of our own making, and a life embodying much good fortune that was not.

Thus, in this bicentennial year, we may not all participate in the festivities with flag-waving fervor. Some may more quietly commemorate the suffering, struggle, and sacrifice that has triumphed over much of what was wrong with the original document, and observe the anniversary with hopes not realized and promises not fulfilled. I plan to celebrate the bicentennial of the Constitution as a living document, including the Bill of Rights and the other amendments protecting individual freedoms and human rights.

CHAPTER 4

The Constitution Later Evaluated, Criticized, and Defended

✴ Chapter Preface

In the more than two centuries since the U.S. Constitution was ratified, many historians and other scholars, as well as politicians and others, have commented on, evaluated, praised, and criticized that pivotal document. In the immediate aftermath of its ratification, for instance, a number of Americans were sure that it would benefit mainly the well-to-do classes, who would, it was feared, have more legal backing than ever to exploit the poor. On the other hand, many others were satisfied that Americans of all walks of life would be well served by the new form of government. That dispute was more or less settled in the course of a generation. As the country began to expand westward, millions of low-income farmers and settlers benefited from exploitation of new lands and resources and/or gained political voices in the new state governments set up in the West.

Other concerns with the Constitution remained, however. Abolitionists complained that it allowed slavery to flourish. And women eventually pointed out (in the women's suffrage movement) that it did not provide them with voting rights. These and several other grievances were addressed in a series of amendments to the Constitution over the years. Still other reexaminations and reevaluations of the Constitution were (and still are) of a more scholarly nature; that is, concerned with its political, economic, and moral underpinnings and the original intent of the framers in creating its provisions.

Regarding the latter group of concerns, perhaps no other single evaluator and critic of the Constitution has been more prominent and controversial than Charles A. Beard. His career, writings, and experiences show how controversial and emotional the intent of a group of men long dead—the Constitution's framers—can be to later generations of Americans. Born in Indiana in 1874, Beard studied history at Oxford University in England. In 1904 he returned to the United States and took a teaching position at Columbia University. As time went on, Beard and his wife got involved in a number of progressive political campaigns, including women's suffrage and the movement to end child labor.

Because he was a frequent vocal critic of the ills of society and the government's frequent reluctance or slowness to address those ills, it is perhaps not surprising that Beard was critical of politicians. In this regard, he did not exclude the Constitution's framers, whom many historians had (sometimes with good reason) placed on a pedestal. In 1913 he published his seminal work, *An Economic Interpretation of the Constitution of the United States.* The book suggests that the founders fashioned the government more to meet their personal economic interests than to acquire liberty for the masses.

Beard paid a heavy price for his stance on the intent of the framers. Although many historians agreed with him fully or in part, many more felt he was way off base. For at least two generations, academic debate raged in American colleges, newspapers, book clubs, and elsewhere over the merits of his thesis. Meanwhile, leading politicians, including President William Howard Taft, roundly attacked Beard, who had clearly exposed a sensitive spot in the American psyche. Moreover, during World War I, American intelligence officials put Beard on a list of individuals deemed "dangerous" to the government because of their progressive leanings. After that he was never again able to secure a teaching post.

Beard died in Connecticut in 1948, leaving an impressive, though highly controversial, legacy in the form of his economic thesis of the Constitution. Numerous full-length books and hundreds of articles have been written either supporting or refuting that thesis, which some scholars continue to debate today. Beard's ideas and personal experiences demonstrate that spirited debate about the Constitution is not a thing of the past, but an ongoing process, part of the relentless struggle of the world's greatest democracy to reexamine, redefine, and thereby improve itself.

Viewpoint 1

"The Framers continue to earn the acclaim of a grateful people, . . . not alone because they ordained and established an enduring constitution, but because they did it in such a resourceful way."

The Constitution Works Thanks to the Founding Fathers

Clinton Rossiter

According to Clinton Rossiter, one of the leading constitutional historians of the twentieth century, the creation of the U.S. Constitution was one of the major events of world history. In his view, which strongly praises the Constitution, the great accomplishments of the United States in the centuries that followed would not have occurred if it had not been for the political genius of the Founding Fathers. After winning their independence from Britain, he says, they had one brief, passing chance to create something the modern world had not yet seen—a national government run by and for the people. They accepted that challenge, Rossiter suggests, and, largely because of their intelligence, talents, and vision, they achieved success beyond even their own wildest dreams, not only for themselves and their children, but for all later American generations.

Clinton Rossiter, *1787: The Grand Convention*. New York: W.W. Norton & Company, 1966. Copyright © 1966 by Clinton Rossiter. Reproduced by permission of the publisher.

A s the delegates set out for home by stage, horseback, or packet (nine of them by way of Congress in New York), their heads were spinning with fatigue and confusion. They could recall where they had begun, and they could see where they had come out; but many must have wondered how they had ever managed to move from the good intentions of May 25 to the sensible conclusions of September 17. As fatigue gave way to composure and cheer, however, so did confusion to understanding, and some of them began to suspect that they had taken part in one of the most purposeful, skilled, and, they hoped, successful meetings of public men in the history of the Western World.

The Nation-Building Instinct

We of a later generation know what they could only suspect: that the Grand Convention was indeed a model gathering of statesmen-politicians, the archetype of the constituent assembly. The Framers continue to earn the acclaim of a grateful people, and also to deserve the attention of a curious world, not alone because they ordained and established an enduring constitution, but because they did it in such a resourceful way. The creation is exemplary; so, too, was the act of creation. Whatever one may think of the Constitution, it would not be easy to imagine a more effective process of constitution-making.

Many of the circumstances under which the Framers had gathered to transact their solemn business were, to be sure, extremely favorable. Their will to succeed was overpowering, nourished as it was by both a sense of the urgency of the hour and a spirit of mission for all mankind; their experience, much of which they had won in common, was exceptional, as was also their learning; their style of political life was self-disciplined, courteous, moderate, and healthily skeptical. They had a sense of the limits of their wisdom, a sense of the limits of the whole endeavor. And they represented, as we have seen, a consensus of principle and purpose that made it possible for them to keep talking across the barricades even in their most gladiatorial moments. Although the struggle for political power was sharp, it was never ferocious or malevolent. Since neither the existence of a religion nor the supremacy of a class nor the fortune of a party was at issue on the floor, the Framers could afford to set their sights on something less than total victory for the states, sections, and interests they represented. Since the process of selection had encouraged only a handful of committed anti-nationalists to appear in Philadelphia—all of whom bowed out before the end—they could abandon the sinking ship of the Confederation with few feelings of guilt or pity. And since the one great interest that lacked the nation-building instinct at this stage of American history—the small farmers of the back country—was only vaguely represented, the troubled leaders of the one great interest that had this instinct in abundance—the merchants and lawyers and planters in the more settled areas—could go about the task of laying a political foundation for the nation with some hope of adjusting their own differences and thus some hope of achieving success. I do not mean to draw too sharp a line between these two interests, in particular to suggest that all yeomen of the West were indifferent or hostile to the nationalist thrust and all gentlemen of the East caught up in it. Yet it must be understood that a majority of the continental elite was ready, for the sake of the Republic and also for the sake of its own power and prosperity, to move rapidly toward nationhood in the 1780's, while a majority of the yeomanry preferred, for the sake of "liberty" and also out of indifference or apathy or antipathy for the elite, to go on as before. If a dozen spokesmen of this interest had shown up in Philadelphia and then stuck to their guns, it is hard to see how James Madison and his friends could have pieced together a nationalist charter.

Effective Use of Committees

Once the Framers had gathered, they thereupon created for themselves, as we have also seen, the best possible circumstances under which to work. Their sessions were orderly but not stagy, decorous but not stilted, flexible but not flighty, secret but not conspiratorial. They worked hard, some almost too hard; and those who remained in Philadelphia attended faithfully. The standard of their debates was high—principally, one suspects, because they were talking only to each other and to posterity—and both long-windedness and irrelevance were at a discount except on a few painful days. The standard of leadership was equally high, and they seemed to know instinctively when to slog ahead blindly, to leave something to chance (which they never did on crucial matters), or to accept guidance from one of their more knowledgeable, committed, or commanding colleagues. Some of the best work of the Convention was done off the floor in private conversations, state caucuses, and informal conferences of like-minded, other-minded, or open-minded men. While the Indian Queen was the focus of this sort of activity, other scenes of discourse and persuasion were Mrs. House's public rooms, the City Tavern, Robert Morris's parlor, Dr. Benjamin Franklin's library, the yard of the State House, the well-paved streets of the city, and the trout stream at Valley Forge.

Perhaps the most impressive aspect of the Convention as a decision-making body was the confident, imaginative, and measured use of committees. At least four were as essential to the process of constitution-making as were the debates on the floor—the self-appointed Virginia caucus of May, the committee of detail, the committee on postponed matters, and the committee of style—and all were manned with delegates well qualified to act creatively for the whole Convention. Two others were essential to the resolution of harsh political problems—the compromising committees of eleven of July 2 and August 22—and they, too, were manned (in the first instance "loaded") to excellent purpose. While the Convention was quite willing to resort to this technique to help it over rough spots—five times in August alone—it did not work it to death, for plenty of "motions to commit" failed to win a majority. And while it gave each committee a confident mandate, it did not propose to swallow the medicine offered without a good look at the prescription. Every report of every committee received the compliment of unruffled scrutiny.

One can think, of course, of small improvements in timing and technique that would have made the Convention an even more effective body. A few less hours might have been spent on the problem of representation and a few more on the judiciary, which was, in a sense, the taken-for-granted stepchild of 1787. There ought, perhaps, to have been some arrangement under which the voluble Luther Martin could be cut off and the silent William Livingston, John Blair, and Robert Morris encouraged to speak. And it cannot be denied that this assembly, like all hard-working assemblies, rolled a little too fast as it neared the end. "It was not exempt," Madison acknowledged in later years, "from a degree of the hurrying influence introduced by fatigue and impatience in all such bodies," and as a result several critical questions went unanswered and several important arrangements unrefined. Yet these, surely, are minor blemishes on a splendid record of both performance and achievement. The political process of the liberal West, it bears repeating, had one of its finest moments in the intense, hard-headed Session of give-and-take among independent gentlemen at Philadelphia in the summer of 1787. Imagined philosopher-kings might have done this work more efficiently than the Framers, but not real men with concrete interests—and with constituents waiting for them at home.

To Strike a Subtle Balance?

Those constituents—the legislators who had sent them, the voters who would elect (and presumably instruct) delegates to the ratifying conventions, the delegates themselves with their power to give or deny life to the Constitution—were much on the minds of the Framers, even in their most detached moments; and the longer the Convention ran, the more forcibly the thought of their constituents pressed upon them. That, of course, is exactly the way things should have been, for they had assembled to write rules not for Athens or Geneva or Utopia, but for the United States of America, an existing country made up of other real men with concrete interests. Since the men had principles as well as interests, and were indeed the most proudly self-governing in the world, the rules had to win the happy approval of the majority, the not unhappy sufferance of the minority, and the unforced obedience of all. At the same time, the Framers were members of an elite, gentlemen who had been taught to lead, although never to bully, and they had no intention of offering a constitution that was simply the lowest common denominator of the wishes, prejudices, and anxieties of the people. Moreover, they could sense that the only half-formed state of opinion in the country would never be more favorable to an imaginative exercise of the arts of political and intellectual leadership.

The search of the Convention, it seems in retrospect, was for solutions that would strike a subtle balance among four principal considerations that framers of constitutions must keep in mind, shifting them about on their personal scales in response to changing pressures of conviction and circumstance. The first is what their constituents have directed them to do, and the Framers were fortunate (or foresighted) enough to have imprecise directions that encouraged them to make the necessary gamble on an entirely new constitution. When William Paterson reminded his colleagues on June 16 that their "object" was "not such a government as may be best in itself, but such a one as our constituents have authorized us to prepare," James Wilson and Edmund Randolph were able to argue plausibly that the Convention, while it was "authorized to *conclude nothing,*" was "at liberty to *propose anything.*"

Anything, they meant to add, that the people would approve, for this is, of course, another principal consideration of would-be framers. The Framers of 1787 never forgot their constituents, "the people of America." "We must consult their rooted prejudices," Nathaniel Gorham advised his colleagues at one critical moment, "if we expect their concurrence in our propositions." "The plan must be accommodated to the public mind," Paterson warned them at another; it must "consult the genius, the temper, the habits, the prejudices of the people." "The genius of the people," George Mason, John Dickinson, and a half-dozen others echoed, commanded republicanism, forbade monarchy, expected bicameralism, and approved the separation of powers. "We must follow the example of Solon," Pierce Butler said in behalf of all his colleagues, "who gave the Athenians not the best government he could devise, but the best they would receive."

The best they would receive, however, was something different from the least they would expect. Throughout the Convention the delegates spoke admiringly of their constituents as men who were rightly tenacious about principles and sensibly flexible about details, and thus as men who were open to explanation and persuasion—especially, it would seem, in the critical area of nationalism. In some things, they recognized, they would have to "follow the people," but in others, they guessed and gambled, the people would follow them. Alexander Hamilton, in particular, was convinced that "the public mind," if properly instructed, would rouse to the challenge of nationhood and "adopt a solid plan."

However they may be instructed, and whatever they may hazard on the probabilities of public opinion, men who would write a long-lived constitution must also worry their heads over the practical question: will it work? Certainly the Framers kept this consideration firmly in mind. They sought not merely immediate approval but continuing viability for their charter, and they got it, one likes to think, because they understood—or came to understand in the course of the summer—what would and would not work in a country with the circumstances, traditions, prospects, and problems of the United States. While some of their attempts to be at all costs "practical" were destined to founder on the shoals of developments they could not anticipate—for example, their ingenious scheme for electing the President—most were to be successful beyond their fondest hopes.

Keeping Faith with the Past

Finally, would-be framers must occasionally raise their eyes above the real to contemplate the ideal, lest their style become that of narrow-minded cynics, and this the Framers of 1787 seemed able to do at the right times and in the right proportion. In a debate of June 22 over the question of how to pay legislators, Randolph sounded one of his truest notes of the summer.

> Mr. Randolph feared we were going too far, in consulting popular prejudices. Whatever respect might be due to them, in lesser matters, or in cases where they formed the permanent character of the people, he thought it, neither incumbent on nor honorable for the Convention to sacrifice right and justice to that consideration.

The choicest story in this vein is one for whose veracity we must rely on the word of Gouverneur Morris. Since Morris told it in "an oration upon the death of General Washington," perhaps we can. Describing the discussions that took place just before the opening of the Convention, Morris saluted the shade of the great man—and drew a stern moral:

> Men of decided temper, who, devoted to the public, over-

looked prudential considerations, thought a form of government should be framed entirely new. But cautious men, with whom popularity was an object, deemed it fit to consult and comply with the wishes of the people. AMERICANS!—let the opinion then delivered by the greatest and best of men, be ever present to your remembrance. He was collected within himself. His countenance had more than usual solemnity— His eye was fixed, and seemed to look into futurity. "It is (said he) too probable that no plan we propose will be adopted. Perhaps another dreadful conflict is to be sustained. If to please the people, we offer what we ourselves disapprove, how can we afterwards defend our work? Let us raise a standard to which the wise and the honest can repair. The event is in the hand of God."—this was the patriot voice of WASHINGTON; and this the constant tenor of his conduct.

The triumph of the Convention of 1787 is that in raising a standard to which the wise and honest could repair, it also raised one that met the threefold test of legitimacy, popularity, and viability.

One reason the Convention was able to strike the right balance between the urge to lead the people and the need to obey them, and between the urge to be noble and the need to be practical, was the disposition of most delegates to be "whole men" on stern principles and "half-way men" on negotiable details. Another was the way in which it worked with familiar materials—the state constitutions, the Articles of Confederation, the best of the colonial experiences—and thus presented the people with a constitution that surprised but did not shock. Rejoicing in philosophy but despising ideology, putting a high value on "reason" but an even higher one on "experience," interested in the institutions of other times and peoples but confident that their own were better, unafraid to contemplate the mysteries of the British Constitution but aware, in Wilson's words, that it "cannot be our own model," the Framers kept faith with the American past even as they prepared to make a break with it. Indeed, the excellence of their handiwork is as much a tribute to their sense of continuity as to their talent for creative statesmanship. The Constitution was an ingenious plan of government chiefly in the sense that its authors made a careful selection of familiar techniques and institutions, then fitted them together with an unerring eye for form. It had very little novelty in it, and that, we see with the aid of hindsight, was one of its strongest points.

A final reason—and also perhaps the most heartening lesson the Convention presents to supporters of constitutional democracy—was the process of give-and-take through which these masterful public men managed to create a constitution that could be carried home with some confidence to every part of a sprawling country. While the process may have often seemed unnecessarily erratic and time-wasting to those trapped in its midst, we can see that it was the only way in which self-respecting representatives of free men could have pieced together a set of operational rules of government and, at the same time, settled their outstanding political differences. In doing these things so well, and so acceptably to all but a handful of their colleagues, the men of 1787 met the supreme test of the democratic assembly: they proved beyond a doubt that the whole was wiser than the parts, that the collective was more creative than any individual in it. No single man, nor even the most artfully constructed team of four or five, could have provided so wisely for the constitutional needs of the American people as did "the cunning of reason" that operated through the whole Convention.

The Convention passed this test and became the archetype of the constituent assembly by acting both negatively and positively to demonstrate its collective wisdom. On one hand, it voted down a string of pet proposals that would have loaded the Constitution with weak, clumsy, or simply unacceptable techniques. Consider, for example, some of the serious suggestions made by serious men to improve the Presidency: Madison wanted to give the Supreme Court a share of the President's veto; Morris favored the Chief Justice as successor to the President; Mason proposed that "maladministration" be added to the list of impeachable offenses; Martin and Elbridge Gerry wanted to fix the size of the army in the Constitution itself; Charles Pinckney would have set a property qualification so high as to bar the Presidency to anyone not as rich as he; and Hugh Williamson agreed with Mason that three executives would be three times as good as one. Every one of these proposals, it should be noted, was thoroughly digested; every one was made, not in the early stages when men were lobbing ideas back and forth for practice, but in the late stages when they were passing on the final plan. Surely the Convention showed itself wiser than these men in rejecting such proposals.

On the other hand, and in a far more important demonstration of the power of collective wisdom, the Convention acted positively to produce those familiar compromises of July 16 and August 25 without which the Union would have collapsed, decayed, or been rent asunder. Especially in the matter of federalism—in drawing the line between nation and states and in adjusting the balance of large states and small—the whole body proved itself more astute than the men who were, in most things, its guiding spirits. If Wilson and Madison had had their way on the issues of representation, the powers of Congress, and the review of state legislation—and they did everything they could to have it—the Constitution could not possibly have won approval in more than a handful of states. By muddling through to "half-way" solutions, and by shaping the solutions to the "genius" of the country as it was interpreted through the prism of a collective mind, the Convention moved up step by step to the outer boundaries of the politically possible in a dozen critical areas, and then refused prudently to move one step beyond. All in all, it was a convincing demonstration of the truth that the highest political wisdom in a constitutional democracy lies in the assembly rather than in the individual lawmaker. The assembly must be of the right size and composition for its purpose, and it must be organized on sound principles and led in a skillful way; but if those conditions are met, as they were met with something to spare in 1787, it has a better chance to find the workable solution than any one man in it.

Looking Back at the Framers

This is not at all to disparage the importance of the individual, for the wisdom of the assembly is of necessity a projection, if not a simple sum, of the wisdom of those who sit in it. The collective triumph of 1787 was nourished on the experience, learning, dedication, and industry of remarkable individuals, and we might therefore end this review of the labors of the Convention by distributing our gratitude and admiration according to the several contributions of the delegates. Although "Ranking the Framers" will never be as popular an indoor sport as "Ranking the Presidents," a student of American history can always play it with pleasure. As I look back once more at all the Framers, limiting my gaze rigidly to their activities between May 14 and September 17, 1787, they seem to fall into eight fairly distinguishable groups, which might be labeled the Principals, the Influentials, the Very Usefuls, the Usefuls, the Visibles, the Ciphers, the Dropouts and Walkouts, and the Inexplicable Disappointments.

The Principals: James Madison. Although even Madison's admiring biographer reminds us that none of the men of 1787 would have dreamed of calling him (or anyone else) the "Father of the Constitution," he was, beyond a doubt, the leading spirit and, as Major Jackson could testify, "most efficient member" in this conclave. His foresight in drafting the Virginia Plan and making it the agenda of the Convention, his willingness to debate great issues and small with courteous and learned intensity, his dozens of suggestions of ways for his colleagues to extricate themselves from thickets, his membership on three of the four essential committees, even perhaps his doggedness in the major struggle for power—these are the solid credentials of the one Framer who stands, modestly and eternally, first among his splendid peers. And as if all these services were not enough, there remains the precious manuscript, written in blood as well as ink, that tells us most of what we know of the Great Happening.

James Wilson, Second only to Madison—and an honorable second—was the learned, inventive, painstaking lawyer from St. Andrews. As brother-in-arms to the Virginian in the cause of reform-minded nationalism, Wilson debated, drafted, bargained, and voted with unremitting zeal. He did most to give strength and independence to the executive, and to lay the foundations of the new government "broad and deep" upon the sovereign people of the United States.

George Washington. Washington's contribution was of a different kind from that of Madison and Wilson, but certainly we can imagine a far less pleasant outcome for a gathering that he had refused to grace or—this, admittedly, is hard to imagine—from which he had withdrawn in sorrow or fury. By lending a constant presence (he did not miss a single day), by presiding with dignity and understanding, by serving willy-nilly as the probable first President, and by giving the quiet support of his influence and vote to Madison, Washington helped mightily to make the Convention a success. Moreover, he did his uncomplaining duty as semi-official chief of state to the American people. He drank tea with the ladies of Philadelphia, dined with the Sons of St. Patrick, visited farms and museums and historic sites, sat through orations, reviewed troops ("at the importunity of General Mifflin"), received visiting dignitaries, and had his portrait painted by Charles Willson Peale. He even went, man of grace and tolerance that he was, "to the Romish Church to high mass."

Gouverneur Morris. The credentials of Gouverneur Morris as a giant of the Convention will always be slightly suspect to those who see him as a man too clever, too fickle, and too cynical "by half." Yet anyone who has traced and retraced his trail through the Convention—noting the frankness and superb timing of his important speeches, watching him shoulder most of the burden of committee work for his fellow Pennsylvanians, reading over his final draft of September 12—must recognize a magnificent contribution. Since the contribution was also quite unexpected, he stands out as the Framer whose reputation received the largest boost in this period. And if he had done nothing else, he would have earned our gratitude for making the Convention chuckle, and also think, with his pointed jokes about overhospitable Indians, hypocritical slavers (the South Carolinians thought, but did not chuckle) and restless Vice-Presidents.

The Influentials: John Rutledge, who spoke often and usefully, sat on five committees, guided the labors of the committee of detail, was the gadfly of the Convention in August and September, and served the cause of moderate nationalism with intelligence and devotion.

Benjamin Franklin, who poked fun along with Morris, spun out compromises and soothed hurt feelings along with the men of Connecticut, spoke up for the people even more confidently than Wilson and Madison, and joined Washington in fortifying both the prestige and the self-confidence of the Convention. (Franklin was one of the few delegates who were sorry to see it all come to an end. "Some tell me I look better," he wrote of his health to his sister, "and they suppose the daily exercise of going and return-ing from the State House has done me good.")

Roger Sherman, probably the most useful and certainly the most voluble delegate from Connecticut, who had a longer intel-lectual pilgrimage to make than any other man in the Convention, and who made it without surrendering a single one of his Yankee principles.

Charles Pinckney, who spoke often and earnestly, and who was at his best filling in the holes of the grand design that was taking shape on the floor.

Rufus King, who turned suddenly, perhaps under the influence of Hamilton, into an enthusiastic, sharp-witted, persuasive nation-alist, and who was the champion committeeman of the summer.

Charles Cotesworth Pinckney, whose single-minded devotion to the interests of his class, state, section, and way of life did not prevent him from lending a powerful hand to the cause of a strong and stable government.

Oliver Ellsworth, the "half-way man" of the century, who may have done more in Philadelphia for the Union than Hamilton, Wilson, and the two Pinckneys together.

Nathaniel Gorham, who chaired the committee of the whole, sat on the committee of detail, and debated helpfully in the spirit of moderate nationalism.

George Mason, unhappily a non-signer, but always a faithful, industrious, honest exponent of old-fashioned republicanism.

Edmund Randolph, also a non-signer, whose performance was erratic, yet who gets considerable credit for the decision to enu-merate the powers of Congress.

Elbridge Gerry, the non-signing "Grumbletonian," who never let the Convention forget that "the genius of the country" was in-deed republican.

The Very Usefuls: John Dickinson, a victim of old age, poor health, and an unfortunate lack of perspective, whose overall per-formance, despite flashes of brilliance, failed to match his consid-erable reputation.

Hugh Williamson, the ablest and hardest-working of the North Carolinians, a member of five committees and a thoughtful par-ticipant in key debates.

William Samuel Johnson, the least talkative but by no means least persuasive member of the Connecticut delegation, who may have had more to do with the success of the committee of style than we think.

George Read, that admirable small-state man with prophetic big-nation ideas.

Pierce Butler, like General Pinckney a little too anxious to serve the interests of those who had sent him, yet also like Pinckney a man worth having in the ranks of the nationalist caucus.

William Paterson, the stubborn and successful advocate of state equality, whose departure in late July may have robbed him of a much higher ranking.

Luther Martin, garrulous, sour, and pigheaded, yet an influential pricker of egos and consciences.

The Usefuls: David Brearly, most faithful of the Jerseyites, supporter of Paterson, and chairman of the committee on postponed matters.

William Livingston, like Dickinson something of a disappointment, who did his best work on committees.

Richard Dobbs Spaight, who had several small triumphs as a plugger of holes.

Gunning Bedford, Jr., who proved explosively that the Framers were not really demigods, and who was an interesting example of the small-state nationalist.

Abraham Baldwin, far and away the best of the Georgians, an able committeeman and a force for intelligent compromise.

Daniel Carroll and John Langdon, each of whom spoke up on two dozen occasions for the cause of moderate nationalism.

William R. Davie, an agent if not an architect of the Great Compromise.

The Visibles: John Blair, who never spoke and never sat on a committee, but whose vote several times provided the margin of victory within the Virginia delegation for Madison and Washington against Mason and Randolph.

Daniel of St. Thomas Jenifer and William Few, who also made their presence felt by voting the right way at critical moments.

Jacob Broom, Caleb Strong, William Houstoun, George Clymer, Jonathan Dayton, and James McHenry, each of whom opened his mouth just often and sensibly enough to catch the ear of history.

James McClurg, who opened it three times, put his foot in twice, and went home to his patients.

The Ciphers: Richard Bassett, who somehow managed to sit through the entire summer without making a speech, serving on a committee, or casting a decisive vote, and who did not make even a single convert to Methodism.

Thomas Mifflin, whose only recorded action was to second a motion of Charles Pinckney.

William Blount and Jared Ingersoll, who spoke up for the first time, and did it feebly, on the last day, and who served on no committees.

Thomas Fitzsimons, Nicholas Gilman, and Alexander Martin, none of whom made any recorded contribution to the proceedings.

The Dropouts and Walkouts: William Churchill Houston, William Pierce, and George Wythe, the last of whom might have been an Influential if fate had permitted him to remain in Philadelphia.

John Francis Mercer, the indignant blade, who could spare the Convention only two weeks and two score ill-tempered observations.

Robert Yates and John Lansing, Jr., the obstinate men from Albany, whose devotion to Governor Clinton forced them to withdraw huffily and rather ingloriously.

The Inexplicable Disappointments: Robert Morris. While in May no one expected the financier to be a Wilson or Madison, in October everyone must have wondered why he had made such a small splash in the proceedings. He had the political and forensic talents, as he had proved in the old days in Congress, to lend a powerful hand to the cause of nationalism, yet he spoke up only twice—to nominate Washington and to second a motion by Read to give Senators a life term—and served on no committee. One can think of many possible explanations for his cipherlike behavior—for example, the pressures of business, the eagerness of his junior colleagues Wilson and Gouverneur Morris, a realization that a new generation was taking over, a desire to mask his vast yet always suspect influence—yet none of them rings quite true.

There must always be something a little pathetic in the contrast of the recorded activities of Robert and Gouverneur Morris. The former made no speeches, which puts him in a class with Blair, Few, Gilman, and Mifflin; the later made 173, which puts him in a class by himself.

Alexander Hamilton. Far and away the most disappointing man was the brilliant New Yorker who had done so much to bring the Convention to life. The wide gap between the possible and the actual in Hamilton's performance at Philadelphia comes as an unpleasant shock to the historian of the Convention, and leads him to wonder if there were not personal reasons for his lackluster showing that have never been revealed. Even when we take into account his eccentric hopes for a high-toned government and his anomalous position on the New York delegation, we are left with the feeling that he could have been a Principal, or at worst an Influential, if he had simply behaved like the man he had been in 1783 or 1786 and was to be again in 1788 and 1790—and even was for a few exciting moments in June and September of 1787. He had so much to give, and he gave so little—that is the cheerless appraisal one is bound to make of Hamilton the Framer. . . .

In the Keeping of the Whole People

It should be plain that some states had rather more to do than others with framing the Constitution of 1787. Every delegation had its moments of glory when it voted for liberty, justice, and union, but not every one played a steady and creative role. Indeed, if we are entirely honest, and prepared to endure the wrath of several state historical societies, we may well conclude that five states—Virginia, Pennsylvania (thanks to the dutiful zeal of three men), Connecticut, South Carolina, and Massachusetts, in that order—produced 95 per cent of the thoughts, decisions, and inventive moments that went into the document, and that the others were largely along for the ride. . . .

In the end, the two dozen truly eminent Framers and the five truly influential states merge into the larger reality of the Grand Convention as a collective, national endeavor. It was healthily collective, as we have seen, because self-propelling individuals gained new wisdom and strength from being thrown together, and went on to build an edifice that no one of them could have built alone. It was healthily national because self-interested states came sooner or later to see that their problems could best be solved, and their existence most effectively guaranteed, by placing the edifice in the keeping of the whole people. The "greatest single effort of national deliberation that the world has ever seen" had led to the discovery of a new kind of nation.

Viewpoint 2

"The Constitution was as democratic as it was because of the influence of popular movements that were a presence, even if not present."

The American People Made the Constitution Successful

Alfred F. Young

A number of modern scholars and other observers of the Constitution agree with historians like Clinton Rossiter that the U.S. Constitution is a great document that has, through its creation of the United States government, changed the world. Unlike Rossiter, however, scholars such as Alfred F. Young, formerly of Northern Illinois University, place less credit for the Constitution's success on the Founding Fathers and more on the people they served. In this essay, Young argues that the founders were mainly wealthy, socially elite gentlemen-farmers who probably would have made the government less democratic if they had possessed the only say in the matter. But they were forced to make compromises that favored democratic principles because of the demands of thousands of ordinary Americans who refused to accept any new government that resembled that of Britain, with whom they had just fought a bloody war of independence.

On June 18, 1787, about three weeks into the Constitutional Convention at Philadelphia, Alexander Hamilton delivered a six-hour address that was easily the longest and most conservative the Convention would hear. Gouverneur Morris, a delegate from Pennsylvania, thought it was "the most able and impressive he had ever heard."

Beginning with the premise that "all communities divide themselves into the few and the many," "the wealthy well born" and "the people," Hamilton added the corollary that the "people are turbulent and changing; they seldom judge or determine right." Moving through history, the delegate from New York developed his ideal for a national government that would protect the few from "the imprudence of democracy" and guarantee "stability and permanence": a president and senate indirectly elected for life ("to serve during good behavior") to balance a house directly elected by a popular vote every three years. This "elective monarch" would have an absolute veto over laws passed by Congress. And the national government would appoint the governors of the states, who in turn would have the power to veto any laws by the state legislatures.

If others quickly saw a resemblance in all of this to the King, House of Lords and House of Commons of Great Britain, with the states reduced to colonies ruled by royal governors, they were not mistaken. The British constitution, in Hamilton's view, remained "the best model the world has ever produced."

Three days later a delegate reported that Hamilton's proposals "had been praised by everybody," but "he has been supported by none." Acknowledging that his plan "went beyond the ideas of most members," Hamilton said he had brought it forward not "as a thing attainable by us, but as a model which we ought to approach as near as possible." When he signed the Constitution the framers finally agreed to on September 17, 1787, Hamilton could accurately say, "no plan was more remote from his own."

Why did the framers reject a plan so many admired? To ask this question is to go down a dark path into the heart of the Constitution few of its celebrants care to take. We have heard so much in our elementary and high school civics books about the "great compromises" within the Convention—between the large states and the small states, between the slaveholders and non-slaveholders, between North and South—that we have missed the much larger accommodation that was taking place between the delegates as a whole at the Convention and what they called "the people out of doors."

The Convention was unmistakably an elite body, . . . weighted with merchants, slaveholding planters and "monied men" who loaned money at interest. Among them were numerous lawyers and college graduates in a country where most men and only a few women had the rudiments of a formal education. They were far from a cross section of the four million or so Americans of that day, most of whom were farmers or artisans, fishermen or sea-men, indentured servants or laborers, half of whom were women and about 600,000 of whom were African-American slaves.

A Short-Range Political Problem

Why did this elite reject Hamilton's plan that many of them praised? James Madison, the Constitution's chief architect, had the nub of the matter. The Constitution was "intended for the ages." To last it had to conform to the "genius" of the American people. "Genius" was a word eighteenth-century political thinkers used to mean spirit: we might say character or underlying values.

James Wilson, second only to Madison in his influence at Philadelphia, elaborated on the idea. "The British government cannot be our model. We have no materials for a similar one. Our manners, our law, the abolition of entail and primogeniture," which made for a more equal distribution of property among sons, "the whole genius of the people, are opposed to it."

This was long-range political philosophy. There was a short-range political problem that moved other realistic delegates in the same direction. Called together to revise the old Articles of Confedera-tion, the delegates instead decided to scrap it and frame an entirely new constitution. It would have to be submitted to the people for ratification, most likely to conventions elected especially for the purpose. Repeatedly, conservatives recoiled from extreme proposals for which they knew they could not win popular support.

In response to a proposal to extend the federal judiciary into the states, Pierce Butler, a South Carolina planter, argued, "the people will not bear such innovations. The states will revolt at such encroachments." His assumption was "we must follow the example of Solon, who gave the Athenians not the best government he could devise but the best they would receive."

The suffrage debate epitomized this line of thinking. Gouverneur Morris, Hamilton's admirer, proposed that the national government limit voting for the House to men who owned a freehold, i.e., a substantial farm, or its equivalent. "Give the vote to people who have no property and they will sell them to the rich who will be able to buy them," he said with some prescience. George Mason, author of Virginia's Bill of Rights, was aghast. "Eight or nine states have extended the right of suffrage beyond the freeholders. What will people there say if they should be disfranchised?"

Benjamin Franklin, the patriarch, speaking for one of the few times in the convention, paid tribute to "the lower class of freemen" who should not be disfranchised. James Wilson explained, "it would be very hard and disagreeable for the same person" who could vote for representatives for the state legislatures "to be excluded from a vote for this in the national legislature." Nathaniel Gorham, a Boston merchant, returned to the guiding principle: "the people will never allow" existing rights to suffrage to be abridged. "We must consult their rooted prejudices if we expect their concurrence in our propositions."

The result? Morris' proposal was defeated and the convention decided that whoever each state allowed to vote for its own assembly could vote for the House. It was a compromise that left the door open and in a matter of decades allowed states to introduce universal white male suffrage.

Making Accommodations to the Past

Clearly there was a process of accommodation at work here. The popular movements of the Revolutionary Era were a presence at the Philadelphia Convention even if they were not present. The delegates, one might say, were haunted by ghosts, symbols of the broadly based movements elites had confronted in the making of the Revolution from 1765 to 1775, in waging the war from 1775 to 1781 and in the years since 1781 within their own states.

The first was the ghost of Thomas Paine, the most influential radical democrat of the Revolutionary Era. In 1776 Paine's pamphlet *Common Sense* (which sold at least 150,000 copies), in arguing for independence, rejected not only King George III but the principle of monarchy and the so-called checks and balances of the unwritten English constitution. In its place he offered a vision of a democratic government in which a single legislature would be supreme, the executive minimal, and representatives would be elected from small districts by a broad electorate for short terms so they could "return and mix again with the voters." John Adams considered *Common Sense* too "democratical," without even an attempt at "mixed government" that would balance "democracy" with "aristocracy."

The second ghost was that of Abraham Yates, a member of the state senate of New York typical of the new men who had risen to power in the 1780s in the state legislatures. We have forgotten him; Hamilton, who was very conscious of him, called him "an old Booby." He had begun as a shoemaker and was a self-taught lawyer and warm foe of the landlord aristocracy of the Hudson Valley which Hamilton had married into. As James Madison identified the "vices of the political system of the United States" in a memorandum in 1787, the Abraham Yateses were the number-one problem. The state legislatures had "an itch for paper money" laws, laws that prevented foreclosure on farm mortgages, and tax laws that soaked the rich. As Madison saw it, this meant that "debtors defrauded their creditors" and "the landed interest has borne hard on the mercantile interest." This, too, is what Hamilton had in mind when he spoke of the "depredations which the democratic spirit is apt to make on property" and what others meant by the "excess of democracy" in the states.

The third ghost was a very fresh one—Daniel Shays. In 1786 Shays, a captain in the Revolution, led a rebellion of debtor farmers in western Massachusetts which the state quelled with its own somewhat unreliable militia. There were "combustibles in every state," as George Washington put it, raising the specter of "Shays-ism." This Madison enumerated among the "vices" of the system as "a want of guaranty to the states against internal violence." Worse still, Shaysites in many states were turning to the political system to elect their own kind. If they succeeded they would produce legal Shaysism, a danger for which the elites had no remedy.

The fourth ghost we can name was the ghost of Thomas Peters, although he had a thousand other names. In 1775, Peters, a Virginia slave, responded to a plea by the British to fight in their army and win their freedom. He served in an "Ethiopian Regiment," some of whose members bore the emblem "Liberty to Slaves" on their uniforms. After the war the British transported Peters and several thousand escaped slaves to Nova Scotia from whence Peters eventually led a group to return to Africa and the colony of Sierra Leone, a long odyssey to freedom. Eighteenth-century slaveholders, with no illusions about happy or contented slaves, were haunted by the specter of slaves in arms.

The Threat of State Democratic Majorities

During the Revolutionary Era elites divided in response to these varied threats from below. One group, out of fear of "the mob" and then "the rabble in arms," embraced the British and became active Loyalists. After the war most of them went into exile. Another group who became patriots never lost their obsession with coercing popular movements. . . .

Far more important, however, were those patriot leaders who adopted a strategy of "swimming with a stream which it is impossible to stem." This was the metaphor of Robert R. Livingston, Jr., . . . a gentleman with a large tenanted estate in New York. Men of his class had to learn to "yield to the torrent if they hoped to direct its course."

Livingston and his group were able to shape New York's constitution, which some called a perfect blend of "aristocracy" and "democracy." John Hancock, the richest merchant in New England, had mastered this kind of politics and emerged as the most popular politician in Massachusetts. In Maryland Charles Carroll, a wealthy planter, instructed his anxious father about the need to "submit to partial losses" because "no great revolution can hap-

pen in a state without revolutions or mutations of private property. If we can save a third of our personal estate and all of our
lands and Negroes, I shall think ourselves well off."

The major leaders at the Constitutional Convention in 1787
were heirs to both traditions: coercion and accommodation—
Hamilton and Gouverneur Morris to the former, James Madison
and James Wilson much more to the latter.

They all agreed on coercion to slay the ghosts of Daniel Shays
and Thomas Peters. The Constitution gave the national government the power to "suppress insurrections" and protect the states
from "domestic violence." There would be a national army under
the command of the president, and authority to nationalize the
state militias and suspend the right of habeas corpus in "cases of
rebellion or invasion." In 1794 Hamilton, as secretary of the treasury, would exercise such powers fully (and needlessly) to suppress the Whiskey Rebellion in western Pennsylvania.

Southern slaveholders correctly interpreted the same powers as
available to shackle the ghost of Thomas Peters. As it turned out,
Virginia would not need a federal army to deal with Gabriel
Prosser's insurrection in 1800 or Nat Turner's rebellion in 1830,
but a federal army would capture John Brown after his raid at
Harpers Ferry in 1859.

But how to deal with the ghosts of Thomas Paine and Abraham
Yates? Here Madison and Wilson blended coercion with accommodation. They had three solutions to the threat of democratic
majorities in the states.

Their first was clearly coercive. Like Hamilton, Madison wanted
some kind of national veto over the state legislatures. He got several very specific curbs on the states written into fundamental law:
no state could "emit" paper money or pass "laws impairing the
obligation of contracts." Wilson was so overjoyed with these two
clauses that he argued that if they alone "were inserted in the Constitution I think they would be worth our adoption."

But Madison considered the overall mechanism adopted to curb
the states "short of the mark." The Constitution, laws and treaties
were the "supreme law of the land" and ultimately a federal court
could declare state laws unconstitutional. But this, Madison
lamented, would only catch "mischiefs" after the fact. Thus they

had clipped the wings of Abraham Yates but he could still fly.

The second solution to the problem of the states was decidedly democratic. They wanted to do an end-run around the state legislatures. The Articles of Confederation, said Madison, rested on "the pillars" of the state legislatures who elected delegates to Congress. The "great fabric to be raised would be more stable and durable if it should rest on the solid grounds of the people themselves"; hence, there would be popular elections to the House.

Wilson altered only the metaphor. He was for "raising the federal pyramid to a considerable altitude and for that reason wanted to give it as broad a base as possible." They would slay the ghost of Abraham Yates with the ghost of Thomas Paine.

This was risky business. They would reduce the risk by keeping the House of Representatives small. Under a ratio of one representative for every 30,000 people, the first house would have only 65 members; in 1776 Thomas Paine had suggested 390. But still, the House would be elected every two years, and with each state allowed to determine its own qualifications for voting, there was no telling who might end up in Congress.

There was also a risk in Madison's third solution to the problem of protecting propertied interests from democratic majorities: "extending the sphere" of government. Prevailing wisdom held that a republic could only succeed in a small geographic area; to rule an "extensive" country, some kind of despotism was considered inevitable.

Madison turned this idea on its head in his since famous *Federalist* essay No. 10. In a small republic, he argued, it was relatively easy for a majority to gang up on a particular "interest." "Extend the sphere," he wrote, and "you take in a greater variety of parties and interests." Then it would be more difficult for a majority "to discover their own strength and to act in unison with each other."

This was a prescription for a non-colonial empire that would expand across the continent, taking in new states as it dispossessed the Indians. The risk was there was no telling how far the "democratic" or "leveling" spirit might go in such likely would-be states as frontier Vermont, Kentucky and Tennessee.

In the spectrum of state constitutions adopted in the Revolutionary Era, the federal Constitution of 1787 was, like New York's, somewhere between "aristocracy" and "democracy." It therefore should not surprise us—although it has eluded many modern critics of the Constitution—that in the contest over ratification in 1787–1788, the democratic minded were divided.

Supporters of Democracy Divided

Among agrarian democrats there was a gut feeling that the Constitution was the work of an old class enemy. "These lawyers and men of learning and monied men," argued Amos Singletary, a working farmer at the Massachusetts ratifying convention, "expect to be managers of this Constitution and get all the power and all the money into their own hands and then will swallow up all of us little folks . . . just as the whale swallowed up Jonah."

Democratic leaders like Melancton Smith of New York focused on the small size of the proposed House. Arguing from Paine's premise that the members of the legislature should "resemble those they represent," Smith feared that "a substantial yeoman of sense and discernment will hardly ever be chosen" and the government "will fall into the hands of the few and the great." Urban democrats, on the other hand, including a majority of the mechanics and tradesmen of the major cities who in the Revolution had been a bulwark of Paineite radicalism, were generally enthusiastic about the Constitution. They were impelled by their urgent stake in a stronger national government that would advance ocean-going commerce and protect American manufacturers from competition. But they would not have been as ardent about the new frame of government without its saving graces. It clearly preserved their rights to suffrage. And the process of ratification, like the Constitution itself, guaranteed them a voice. As early as 1776 the New York Committee of Mechanics held it as "a right which God has given them in common with all men to judge whether it be consistent with their interest to accept or reject a constitution."

Mechanics turned out en masse in the parades celebrating ratification, marching trade by trade. The slogans and symbols they carried expressed their political ideals. In New York the upholsterers had a float with an elegant "Federal Chair of State" flanked by the symbols of Liberty and Justice that they identified with the

Constitution. In Philadelphia the bricklayers put on their banner "Both buildings and rulers are the work of our hands."

Democrats who were skeptical found it easier to come over because of the Constitution's redeeming features. Thomas Paine, off in Paris, considered the Constitution "a copy, though not quite as base as the original, of the form of the British government." He had always opposed a single executive and he objected to the "long duration of the Senate." But he was so convinced of "the absolute necessity" of a stronger federal government that "I would have voted for it myself had I been in America or even for a worse, rather than have none." It was crucial to Paine that there was an amending process, the means of "remedying its defects by the same appeal to the people by which it was to be established."

Elites Shaped by Popular Movements?

In drafting the Constitution in 1787 the framers, self-styled Federalists, made their first accommodation with the "genius" of the people. In campaigning for its ratification in 1788 they made their second. At the outset, the conventions in the key states—Massachusetts, New York and Virginia—either had an anti-Federalist majority or were closely divided. To swing over a small group of "antis" in each state, Federalists had to promise that they would consider amendments. This was enough to secure ratification by narrow margins in Massachusetts, 187 to 168; in New York, 30 to 27; and in Virginia, 89 to 79.

What the anti-Federalists wanted were dozens of changes in the structure of the government that would cut back national power over the states, curb the powers of the presidency as well as protect individual liberties. What they got was far less. But in the first Congress in 1789, James Madison, true to his pledge, considered all the amendments and shepherded 12 amendments through both houses. The first two of these failed in the states; one would have enlarged the House. The 10 that were ratified by December 1791 were what we have since called the Bill of Rights, protecting freedom of expression and the rights of the accused before the law. Abraham Yates considered them "trivial and unimportant." But other democrats looked on them much more favorably. In time the limited meaning of freedom of speech in the First Amendment was broadened far beyond the framers' original intent. Later popular movements thought of the Bill of Rights as an essential part of the "constitutional" and "republican" rights that belonged to the people.

There is a cautionary tale here that surely goes beyond the process of framing and adopting the Constitution and Bill of Rights from 1787 to 1791. The Constitution was as democratic as it was because of the influence of popular movements that were a presence, even if not present. The losers helped shape the results. We owe the Bill of Rights to the opponents of the Constitution, as we do many other features in the Constitution put in to anticipate opposition.

In American history popular movements often shaped elites, especially in times of crisis when elites were concerned with the "system." Elites have often divided in response to such threats and according to their perception of the "genius" of the people. Some have turned to coercion, others to accommodation. We run serious risk if we ignore this distinction.

Viewpoint 3

"[The Constitution] was an economic document drawn with superb skill by men whose property interests were immediately at stake."

The Founders Shaped the Constitution to Secure Their Own Economic Interests

Charles A. Beard

Probably the most influential modern reevaluation of the U.S. Constitution was that of former Columbia University scholar Charles A. Beard. In his 1913 book, *An Economic Interpretation of the Constitution*, he argued that the Founding Fathers, though well-meaning, were motivated more by selfish interest than anything else when they were drawing up the blueprint for the new national government. This controversial interpretation of the Constitution sparked heated debate that continues in some circles to the present. In the following excerpts from his masterwork, Beard makes the point that James Madison and other framers repeatedly stressed the importance of maintaining and perpetuating property rights; and after all, these men were the country's social, as well as political, elite, who owned most of the

Charles A. Beard, *An Economic Interpretation of the Constitution.* New York: Macmillan, 1913.

valuable property and wanted to pass it on to their heirs. This naturally set them apart from their less-well-off countrymen. "Class and group divisions based on property lie at the basis of modern government," Beard wrote, "and politics and constitutional law are inevitably a reflex of these contending interests."

The inquiry which follows is based upon the political science of James Madison, the father of the Constitution and later President of the Union he had done so much to create. This political science runs through all of his really serious writings and is formulated in its most precise fashion in *The Federalist* as follows: "The diversity in the faculties of men, from which the rights of property originate, is not less an insuperable obstacle to a uniformity of interests. The protection of these faculties is the first object of government. From the protection of different and unequal faculties of acquiring property, the possession of different degrees and kinds of property immediately results; and from the influence of these on the sentiments and views of the respective proprietors, ensues a division of society into different interests and parties. . . . The most common and durable source of factions has been the various and unequal distribution of property. Those who hold and those who are without property have ever formed distinct interests in society. Those who are creditors, and those who are debtors, fall under a like discrimination. A landed interest, a manufacturing interest, a mercantile interest, a moneyed interest, with many lesser interests, grow up of necessity in civilized nations and divide them into different classes, actuated by different sentiments and views. The regulation of these various and interfering interests forms the principal task of modern legislation, and involves the spirit of party and faction in the necessary and ordinary operations of the government."

Here we have a masterly statement of the theory of economic determinism in politics. Different degrees and kinds of property inevitably exist in modern society; party doctrines and "principles" originate in the sentiments and views which the possession of various kinds of property creates in the minds of the possessors; class and group divisions based on property lie at the basis of modern government; and politics and constitutional law are inevitably a reflex of these contending interests. Those who are inclined to repudiate the hypothesis of economic determinism as a European importation must, therefore, revise their views, on learning that one of the earliest, and certainly one of the clearest, statements of it came from a profound student of politics who sat in the Convention that framed our fundamental law.

An Economic Biography

The requirements for an economic interpretation of the formation and adoption of the Constitution may be stated in a hypothetical proposition which, although it cannot be verified absolutely from ascertainable data, will at once illustrate the problem and furnish a guide to research and generalization.

It will be admitted without controversy that the Constitution was the creation of a certain number of men, and it was opposed by a certain number of men. Now, if it were possible to have an economic biography of all those connected with its framing and adoption,—perhaps about 160,000 men altogether,—the materials for scientific analysis and classification would be available. Such an economic biography would include a list of the real and personal property owned by all of these men and their families: lands and houses, with incumbrances, money at interest, slaves, capital invested in shipping and manufacturing, and in state and continental securities.

Suppose it could be shown from the classification of the men who supported and opposed the Constitution that there was no line of property division at all; that is, that men owning substantially the same amounts of the same kinds of property were equally divided on the matter of adoption or rejection—it would then become apparent that the Constitution had no ascertainable relation to economic groups or classes, but was the product of some abstract causes remote from the chief business of life—gaining a livelihood.

Suppose, on the other hand, that substantially all of the merchants, money lenders, security holders, manufacturers, shippers, capitalists, and financiers and their professional associates are to be found on one side in support of the Constitution and that substantially all or the major portion of the opposition came from the non-slaveholding farmers and the debtors—would it not be pretty conclusively demonstrated that our fundamental law was not the product of an abstraction known as "the whole people," but of a group of economic interests which must have expected beneficial results from its adoption? Obviously all the facts here desired cannot be discovered, but the data . . . bear out the latter hypothesis, and thus a reasonable presumption in favor of the theory is created.

Of course, it may be shown (and perhaps can be shown) that the farmers and debtors who opposed the Constitution were, in fact, benefited by the general improvement which resulted from its adoption. It may likewise be shown, to take an extreme case, that the English nation derived immense advantages from the Norman Conquest and the orderly administrative processes which were introduced, as it undoubtedly did; nevertheless, it does not follow that the vague thing known as "the advancement of general welfare" or some abstraction known as "justice" was the immediate, guiding purpose of the leaders in either of these great historic changes. The point is, that the direct, impelling motive in both cases was the economic advantages which the beneficiaries expected would accrue to themselves first, from their action. Further than this, economic interpretation cannot go. It may be that some larger world-process is working through each series of historical events: but ultimate causes lie beyond our horizon. . . .

The First Concern of Government

Before taking up the economic implications of the structure of the federal government, it is important to ascertain what, in the opinion of *The Federalist*, is the basis of all government. The most philosophical examination of the foundations of political science is made by Madison in the tenth number. Here he lays down, in no uncertain language, the principle that the first and elemental concern of every government is economic.

1. "The first object of government," he declares, is the protection of "the diversity in the faculties of men, from which the rights of property originate." The chief business of government, from which, perforce, its essential nature must be derived, consists in the control and adjustment of conflicting economic interests. Af-

ter enumerating the various forms of propertied interests which spring up inevitably in modern society, he adds: "The regulation of these various and interfering interests forms the principal task of modern legislation, and involves the spirit of party and faction in the ordinary operations of the government."

2. What are the chief causes of these conflicting political forces with which the government must concern itself? Madison answers. Of course fanciful and frivolous distinctions have sometimes been the cause of violent conflicts; "but the most common and durable source of factions has been the various and unequal distribution of property. Those who hold and those who are without property have ever formed distinct interests in society. Those who are creditors, and those who are debtors, fall under a like discrimination. A landed interest, a manufacturing interest, a mercantile interest, a moneyed interest, with many lesser interests grow up of necessity in civilized nations, and divide them into different classes actuated by different sentiments and views."

3. The theories of government which men entertain are emotional reactions to their property interests. "From the protection of different and unequal faculties of acquiring property, the possession of different degrees and kinds of property immediately results; *and from the influence of these on the sentiments and views of the respective proprietors, ensues a division of society into different interests and parties.*" Legislatures reflect these interests. "What," he asks, "are the different classes of legislators but advocates and parties to the causes which they determine." There is no help for it. "The causes of faction cannot be removed," and "we well know that neither moral nor religious motives can be relied on as an adequate control."

4. Unequal distribution of property is inevitable, and from it contending factions will rise in the state. The government will reflect them, for they will have their separate principles and "sentiments"; but the supreme danger will arise from the fusion of certain interests into an overbearing majority, which Madison, in another place, prophesied would be the landless proletariat,—an overbearing majority which will make its "rights" paramount, and sacrifice the "rights" of the minority. "To secure the public good," he declares, "and private rights against the danger of such a fac-

tion and at the same time preserve the spirit and the form of popular government is then the great object to which our inquiries are directed."

5. How is this to be done? Since the contending classes cannot be eliminated and their interests are bound to be reflected in politics, the only way out lies in making it difficult for enough contending interests to fuse into a majority, and in balancing one over against another. The machinery for doing this is created by the new Constitution and by the Union. (*a*) Public views are to be refined and enlarged "by passing them through the medium of a chosen body of citizens." (*b*) The very size of the Union will enable the inclusion of more interests so that the danger of an overbearing majority is not so great. "The smaller the society, the fewer probably will be the distinct parties and interests composing it; the fewer the distinct parties and interests, the more frequently will a majority be found of the same party. . . . Extend the sphere, and you take in a greater variety of parties and interests; you make it less probable that a majority of the whole will have a common motive to invade the rights of other citizens; or if such a common motive exists, it will be more difficult for all who feel it to discover their strength and to act in unison with each other.". . .

"In the extent and proper structure of the Union, therefore, we behold a republican remedy for the diseases most incident to republican government."

How to Keep the Government in Close Rein

The fundamental theory of political economy thus stated by Madison was the basis of the original American conception of the balance of powers which is formulated at length in four numbers of *The Federalist* and consists of the following elements:

1. No mere parchment separation of departments of government will be effective. "The legislative department is everywhere extending the sphere of its activity, and drawing all power into its impetuous vortex. The founders of our republic . . . seem never for a moment to have turned their eyes from the danger to liberty from the overgrown and all-grasping prerogative of an hereditary magistrate, supported and fortified by an hereditary branch of the legislative authority. They seem never to have recollected the dan-

ger from legislative usurpations, which, by assembling all power in the same hands, must lead to the same tyranny as is threatened by executive usurpations."

2. Some sure mode of checking usurpations in the government must be provided, other than frequent appeals to the people. "There appear to be insuperable objections against the proposed recurrence to the people as a provision in all cases for keeping the several departments of power within their constitutional limits." In a contest between the legislature and the other branches of the government, the former would doubtless be victorious on account of the ability of the legislators to plead their cause with the people.

3. What then can be depended upon to keep the government in close rein? "The only answer that can be given is, that as all these exterior provisions are found to be inadequate, the defect must be supplied by so contriving the interior structure of the government as that its several constituent parts may, by their mutual relations, be the means of keeping each other in their proper places. . . . It is of great importance in a republic not only to guard the society against the oppression of its rulers, but to guard one part of the society against the injustice of the other part. Different interests necessarily exist in different classes of citizens. If a majority be united by a common interest, the rights of the minority will be insecure." There are two ways of obviating this danger: one is by establishing a monarch independent of popular will, and the other is by reflecting these contending interests (so far as their representatives may be enfranchised) in the very structure of the government itself so that a majority cannot dominate the minority—which minority is of course composed of those who possess property that may be attacked. "Society itself will be broken into so many parts, interests, and classes of citizens, that the rights of individuals, or of the minority, will be in little danger from interested combinations of the majority."

4. The structure of the government as devised at Philadelphia reflects these several interests and makes improbable any danger to the minority from the majority. "The House of Representatives being to be elected immediately by the people, the Senate by the State legislatures, the President by electors chosen for that purpose by the people, there would be little probability of a common

interest to cement these different branches in a predilection for any particular class of electors."

5. All of these diverse interests appear in the amending process but they are further reinforced against majorities. An amendment must receive a two-thirds vote in each of the two houses so constituted and the approval of three-fourths of the states.

6. The economic corollary of this system is as follows: Property interests may, through their superior weight in power and intelligence, secure advantageous legislation whenever necessary, and they may at the same time obtain immunity from control by parliamentary majorities.

If we examine carefully the delicate instrument by which the framers sought to check certain kinds of positive action that might be advocated to the detriment of established and acquired rights, we cannot help marvelling at their skill. Their leading idea was to break up the attacking forces at the starting point: the source of political authority for the several branches of the government. This disintegration of positive action at the source was further facilitated by the differentiation in the terms given to the respective departments of the government. And the crowning counterweight to "an interested and over-bearing majority," as Madison phrased it, was secured in the peculiar position assigned to the judiciary, and the use of the sanctity and mystery of the law as a foil to democratic attacks. . . .

No Direct Attacks on Property

These are the great powers conferred on the new government: taxation, war, commercial control, and disposition of western lands. Through them public creditors may be paid in full, domestic peace maintained, advantages obtained in dealing with foreign nations, manufactures protected, and the development of the territories go forward with full swing. The remaining powers are minor and need not be examined here. What implied powers lay in the minds of the framers likewise need not be inquired into; they have long been the subject of juridical speculation.

None of the powers conferred by the Constitution on Congress permits a direct attack on property. The government is given no general authority to define property. It may tax, but indirect taxes must be uniform, and these are to fall upon consumers. Direct taxes may be laid, but resort to this form of taxation is rendered practically impossible, save on extraordinary occasions, by the provision that they must be apportioned according to population—so that numbers cannot transfer the burden to accumulated wealth. The slave trade may be destroyed, it is true, after the lapse of a few years; but slavery as a domestic institution is better safeguarded than before. . . .

Equally important to personalty as the positive powers conferred upon Congress to tax, support armies, and regulate commerce were the restrictions imposed on the states. Indeed, we have the high authority of Madison for the statement that of the forces which created the Constitution, those property interests seeking protection against omnipotent legislatures were the most active.

In a letter to Jefferson, written in October, 1787, Madison elaborates the principle of federal judicial control over state legislation, and explains the importance of this new institution in connection with the restrictions laid down in the Constitution on laws affecting private rights. "The mutability of the laws of the States," he says, "is found to be a serious evil. The injustice of them has been so frequent and so flagrant as to alarm the most steadfast friends of Republicanism. I am persuaded I do not err in saying that the evils issuing from these sources contributed more to that uneasiness which produced the Convention, and prepared the public mind for a general reform, than those which accrued to our national character and interest from the inadequacy of the Confederation to its immediate objects. A reform, therefore, which does not make provision for private rights must be materially defective."

Two small clauses embody the chief demands of personalty against agrarianism: the emission of paper money is prohibited and the states are forbidden to impair the obligation of contract. The first of these means a return to a specie basis—when coupled with the requirement that the gold and silver coin of the United States shall be the legal tender. The Shays and their paper money legions,[1] who assaulted the vested rights of personalty by the pro-

1. Daniel Shays led a rebellion against the state of Massachusetts after the state refused to provide economic aid to farmers.

cess of legislative depreciation, are now subdued forever, and money lenders and security holders may be sure of their operations. Contracts are to be safe, and whoever engages in a financial operation, public or private, may know that state legislatures cannot destroy overnight the rules by which the game is played.

A principle of deep significance is written in these two brief sentences. The economic history of the states between the Revolution and the adoption of the Constitution is compressed in them. They appealed to every money lender, to every holder of public paper, to every man who had any personalty at stake. The intensity of the economic interests reflected in these two prohibitions can only be felt by one who has spent months in the study of American agrarianism after the Revolution. In them personalty won a significant battle in the conflict of 1787–1788 [Shays rebellion]. . . .

The Spirit of Commerce

The authors of *The Federalist* carry over into the field of international politics the concept of economic antagonisms which lie at the basis of their system of domestic politics. Modern wars spring primarily out of commercial rivalry, although the ambitions of princes have often been a source of international conflict. "Has commerce hitherto done anything more than change the objects of war?" asks [Alexander] Hamilton. "Is not the love of wealth as domineering and enterprising a passion as that of power or glory? Have there not been as many wars founded upon commercial motives, since that has become the prevailing system of nations, as were before occasioned by the cupidity of territory or dominion? Has not the spirit of commerce, in many instances, administered new incentives to the appetite, both for the one and for the other?" Let history answer. Carthage, a commercial republic, was an aggressor in a war that ended in her destruction. The furious contests of Holland and England were over the dominion of the sea. Commerce has been for ages the predominant pursuit of England, and she has been constantly engaged in wars. . . .

In this world-wide and age-long conflict of nations for commercial advantages, the United States cannot expect to become a non-resistant, an idle spectator. Even were pacific ideals to dominate American policy, she could not overcome the scruples of her ambitious rivals. In union, therefore, is strength against aggression and in support of offensive operations. Moreover, the Union will be better able to settle disputes amicably because of the greater show of power which it can make. "Acknowledgements, explanations, and compensations are often accepted as satisfactory from a strong united nation, which would be rejected as unsatisfactory if offered by a state or a confederacy of little consideration or power."

Turning from the material causes of foreign wars the authors of *The Federalist* examine the possible sources of danger from domestic discord among the states, regarded as independent sovereignties. And how may such domestic discord arise? . . .

Lust for power and dominion, the desire for equality and safety, the ambitions of leaders. Has it not invariably been found [Hamilton asks] "that momentary passions, and immediate interests have a more active and imperious control over human conduct than general and remote considerations of policy, utility, or justice? . . . Has commerce hitherto done anything more than change the objects of war? Is not the love of wealth as domineering and enterprizing a passion as that of power or glory? Have there not been as many wars founded upon commercial motives since that has become the prevailing system of nations, as were before occasioned by the cupidity of territory or dominion?". . . .

Potential Conflict Among the States

Turning from the question as to the extent of the economic motive in the personal element, Hamilton makes an inquiry into the more probable sources of wars among the states in case a firmer union, endowed with adequate powers, is not established. These he enumerates:

1. "Territorial disputes have at all times been found one of the most fertile sources of hostility among nations." The several states have an interest in the Western Territories, and "to reason from the past to the future, we shall have good ground to apprehend that the sword would sometimes be appealed to as the arbiter of their differences."

2. "The competitions of commerce would be another fruitful source of contention." Each state will pursue a policy conducive to its own advantage, and "the spirit of enterprize, which charac-

terizes the commercial part of America, has left no occasion of displaying itself unimproved. It is not at all probable that this unbridled spirit would pay much respect to those regulations of trade by which particular states might endeavor to secure exclusive benefits to their own citizens." The economic motive will thus probably override all considerations of interstate comity and all considerations of international law. But that is not all; says Hamilton, in italics, "*We should be ready to denominate injuries those things which were in reality the justifiable acts of independent sovereignties consulting a distinct interest.*" Commerce will have little respect for the right of other peoples to protect their interests, and it will stigmatize as an "injury" anything which blocks its enterprise.

3. "The public debt of the Union would be a further cause of collision between the separate states or confederacies." Some states would oppose paying the debt. Why? Because they are "less impressed with the importance of national credit, or because their citizens have little, if any, immediate interest in the question." But other states, "a numerous body of whose citizens are creditors to the public beyond the proportion of the state in the total amount of the national debt, would be strenuous for some equitable and effective provision." In other words, citizens who had nothing at stake would be indifferent, and those who had something to lose would clamor. Foreign powers also might intervene, and the "double contingency of external invasion and internal contention" would be hazarded.

4. "Laws in violation of private contracts, as they amount to aggressions on the rights of those states whose citizens are injured by them, may be considered as another probable source of hostility." Had there not been plenty of evidence to show that state legislatures, if unrestrained by some higher authority, would attack private rights in property? And had there not been a spirit of retaliation also? "We reasonably infer that in similar cases, under other circumstances, a war, not of *parchment*, but of the sword, would chastise such atrocious breaches of moral obligation and social justice."

These, then, are the four leading sources of probable conflict among the states if not united into a firm union: territory, commerce, the national debt, and violations of contractual rights in property—all as severely economic as could well be imagined.

To carry the theory of the economic interpretation of the Constitution out into its ultimate details would require a monumental commentary, such as lies completely beyond the scope of this volume. But enough has been said to show that the concept of the Constitution as a piece of abstract legislation reflecting no group interests and recognizing no economic antagonisms is entirely false. It was an economic document drawn with superb skill by men whose property interests were immediately at stake; and as such it appealed directly and unerringly to identical interests in the country at large.

Viewpoint 4

"Without denying that economics may have been important, the political motives of the delegates must be included to establish the context within which they acted."

The Motivation for Creating the Constitution Was More Political than Economic

David G. Smith

In this essay, Swarthmore College scholar David G. Smith, author of *The Convention and the Constitution: The Political Ideas of the Founding Fathers*, counters the influential thesis of Charles A. Beard, namely that the founders shaped the Constitution in large part to protect their personal property and other economic interests. Smith concedes Beard's point that the men who framed the country's new government did benefit economically from the structure of that government; however, says Smith, this outcome was incidental to other considerations, most of

David G. Smith, *The Convention and the Constitution: The Political Ideas of the Founding Fathers.* New York: St. Martin's Press, 1965. Copyright © 1965 by St. Martin's Press, Inc. Reproduced by permission.

them mainly political in nature. "Their speeches and their language," he writes, "do not support an interpretation that they wanted primarily to defeat democracy or erect an anti-popular oligarchy." Instead, according to Smith, the framers were motivated mostly by a desire to create a lasting legacy of fair government and a strong Union that would stand the test of time.

C onstitution-worship was profaned early in the twentieth century by a generation led by the historians Charles Beard and J. Allen Smith. According to Beard, who wrote the most controversial interpretation of the Convention, the Constitution was not the fruition of Anglo-Saxon liberty; still less was it an impartial judicial instrument protecting the good of all. Behind "justice" and "the Constitution," Beard saw groups of men and economic interest, even a hint of conspiracy. The Constitution, he said, was not the creation of disinterested patriots, nor did it represent the will of the whole people. The men who drafted the Constitution had personal pecuniary interests. The adoption of the Constitution also was originated and accomplished principally by "four groups of personalty interests which had been adversely affected under the Articles of Confederation: money, public securities, manufactures, trading and shipping.". . .

The Political Objectives of the Delegates

Whether right or wrong, Beard's interpretation of the Convention has been enormously influential. It shocked some and comforted others of the Wilsonian era, and was almost received doctrine during the New Deal [the era of the 1930s]. Historians and political scientists have continued to this day to reinterpret the Convention and to quarrel with Beard and his spiritual kinsmen.

The alleged economic motivations or antidemocratic intent of the Founding Fathers, even if the allegations are true, do not rob the Constitution of legitimacy nor destroy the importance of the political theory underlying it. For whatever the intent, the result stands independently. The dispute over original intentions has, however, directed attention away from the larger principles of the

Constitution to an inconclusive debate over the interests, motives, and group loyalties of the Founding Fathers. For this reason, alternate interpretations of the delegates' motives, or different ways of looking at the same facts are important to an understanding of the Constitution itself.

Beard argued that the motivation of the Founding Fathers and of the supporters of the Constitution was principally economic. Yet the men who made the Constitution, and many who were active—either for or against ratification—had also serious political motivations. Without denying that economics may have been important, the political motives of the delegates must be included to establish the context within which they acted. In some instances the latter motives were, properly, separable from the economic, and in some instances they were directed toward larger and more inclusive objectives than the economic ones.

[Some scholars] have stressed the antidemocratic intent of the delegates and compared the Convention and the adoption to a counter-revolution. But they paid little attention to the society for which the Constitution was made. In fact, the political objectives of the delegates were sensible ones, given the society in which they lived.

The main issue with Beard . . . and other idol-smashers . . . is the interpretation of the acts of the delegates. Interpretation depends upon context; and an alternate interpretation depends upon enlarging the context within which the delegates acted. That enlarged context is the "disharmonious society" for which the Constitution was made. That context does not destroy the anti-Convention indictment. It simply demonstrates that the indictment can be subsumed as incidental to a bigger purpose: to erect a large political edifice upon weak constitutional foundations.

We return briefly to the eighteenth-century society [of the founders]. . . . The society was disharmonious because it tended toward group and sectional particularism, and because the political attitudes needed to support common republican government were not firmly set nor strongly entrenched. There were few of the moderating influences that we associate with democracy in modern, urban, and industrialized societies: intersectional ties, a national economy, and a wide sharing and communication of common political attitudes. Eighteenth-century society, furthermore, lacked many of the institutional resources with which to create a "reasonable" or "moderate" politics, to borrow the language of that time. Parties were loose factional assemblages; and political communication was poorly organized. Under all these circumstances, and despite all that worked in favor of republican government, the danger of expanding or "cumulative" political conflict was a very real, if not always present, threat.

The language of the delegates in Convention supports a view that they were primarily concerned with creating a constitution for a "disharmonious society" lacking adequate supports for a moderate federal republic. Their speeches and their language do not support an interpretation that they wanted primarily to defeat democracy or erect an anti-popular oligarchy. In the florid oratory of the opening days of the Convention the delegates denounced the democratic provisions of the Articles and of the state constitutions, the rage for paper money, and the unreasonableness of the people. But for the most part, they spoke of different fears: of cabal and faction; of dissolution or consolidation; of monarchy or popular upheaval. They were fearful mainly not of democracy or attacks upon property, but of continuing, unchecked tendencies to an extreme, and of political expressions that would undermine republican government itself.

Indifferent to State Politics?

The constitution the delegates constructed indicates also that, whatever may have been their other concerns, they were fundamentally engaged in an attempt to strengthen the American polity so that the future republican government could function effectively. Their strategy—logical under the circumstances—included three principal methods or aims. One was to withdraw especially fruitful sources of contention from the most quarrelsome and heated centers of political dispute and thereby limit a tendency toward cumulative political conflict. Another technique of the delegates was to strengthen both the political and nonpolitical bonds of unity. And lastly, also in keeping with rational strategy under prevalent political conditions, they sought to create an artificial frame of government to limit and to sublimate the natural tendencies of politics in their "disharmonious society."

The delegates withdrew power from the states; especially they withdrew some principal objects of political contention from the reach of local democracy. The Constitution prohibited interference with contracts or with commerce among the states. It also enjoined each state to grant "full faith and credit" to the public acts, records, and judicial proceedings of other states and to recognize for the citizens of each state the "privileges and immunities" of citizens in the several states.

By one account, in these provisions the delegates acted to limit democracy and to protect property. By another, they attempted to remove sources of contention from the power of the states, to provide for a national citizenship and for a new government with power to act as representative and trustee of citizens possessed of a dual citizenship.

Actually, the delegates in Convention seemed to be relatively indifferent to the *internal* politics of the states. They did not consistently take the side of debtors or creditors, democrats or oligarchs. Nor did they appear to fear local democracy as such. They did not care, either, how many heads were broken on the local level. But they were intensely and continuously concerned with political conflict that weakened the union, undermined a growing nationhood, or threatened the stability of a republican government.

Aside from the provisions cited and those designed to secure national control of foreign relations, the states were left substantially in charge of their own affairs. They retained their traditional police power almost in its entirety, along with control over property, crime, civil injuries, and social arrangements. The delegates removed from the states very little. Indeed, to have done so would have, in their view, both threatened to create a monarchy, centralized discontent, and made the common government itself too much subject to contention. Instead, they sought to create an additional tier of government and a new constituency principally to defend and represent what citizens enjoyed in common as Americans.

Those objects of political controversy that the delegates sought to protect from the states were critical in amending the major defects of their disharmonious society. A national commerce and protection of common rights would contribute both to a national citizenship and to removing causes of dissension among the states. Their protection would encourage both political and economic growth. And by putting them out of the reach of the states and local governments, some of the heat would be removed from a politics that tended dangerously toward cumulative and uncontrollable conflict.

The Bonds of Union

Aside from an attempt to withdraw certain subjects of contention from state action, the delegates were also especially concerned to strengthen the bonds of union. The contract and commerce clauses, indeed all of those clauses of the Constitution that deal with property, need to be read in this context. The delegates set up protections for property, for commerce, and for sound money. They particularly sought to protect the foundations upon which personalty and economic endeavor rested. To follow the delegates in Convention is revealing. They discuss property, the commerce clause, and conflicts of debtors and creditors. But they talked directly about these matters very little. They are discussed almost wholly in conjunction with *other* objects: navigation acts, the slave trade, the burden of taxation, etc.

Property found its place among many other interests, and especially as an adjunct to *political* objectives such as military strength and corporate unity, or *social* objectives such as access to unappropriated resources and equality of status. Usually, the delegates seemed primarily interested in settling upon one or another social or political objective. The battles in the Convention about these interests or ends were often fierce. When agreement was reached, economic arrangements appeared to follow pretty much as a matter of course and even of indifference. Often they were simply taken over from some clause in the Articles, or from a practice made familiar by their colonial experience. One may say, then, that economic and property arrangements were subordinate to the interests of federal union, political stability, and the future economic and social development within the United States. The delegates adopted those property arrangements they felt would conduce the long-term interests of the nation they saw growing from their efforts.

Property was protected; and a measure of control over property and especially personalty was withdrawn from the states. The delegates may have incidentally benefited the interests of creditors or merchants or speculators. In fact, they did not seem specifically to want to protect them. In any case, they had other ends. One was withdrawing a source of controversy from direct political action by the states. The delegates were also filling out and giving specific character to a conception of national citizenship and of future national development. And they were, finally, artificially strengthening the polity by associating union and common republican government with economic advantage and development.

"Remedies" to Popular Democracy

The delegates' treatment of democracy, or popular government, probably appears by contemporary standards the most suspect of all their deeds. Notice again, however, that an interpretation of their actions depends upon the context in which they are read. Their actions could have been aimed at weakening democracy. They could also have been intended to strengthen artificially a republican government under circumstances requiring precisely that approach to secure a popular government on a national scale. The delegates sought to erect a national government. They sought to establish a dual citizenship under which people would be at once members of a locale and of a state, but would share in a joint venture of federal and republican government. They created scope for an additional layer or level of government, an independent government with its own machinery of courts, its own taxing powers, and a capacity to develop loyalties. They knew the tendencies of the politics of their time. Consequently, they sought equally to guard against the most dangerous tendencies of the government they were creating.

The Founding Fathers called themselves supporters of republican government, by which they meant representative government, derived from the great bulk of the people, but so arranged as to secure stability and government of the wise and virtuous. They meant by "wise and virtuous" primarily wise in the ways of politics and filled with republican virtue. The delegates understood from their own experience that the government, to work at all, required political leaders at the national level with considerable dis-interested devotion to the republic. Remember their experience: their enormous efforts and great difficulty in getting the project started and their many frustrations. They had seen how readily jeal-ousies could set individuals and sections against each other. From their experience—under colonial governments, during the Revo-lution, under the Articles—they knew that a stratum of patriots was not only a necessary support to government, but a needed se-curity against factionalism, cabal, or disruptive parochialism.

A prime objective of the Convention was, therefore, to provide for moderate and independent leadership for the nation in spite of the masses or popular majorities, especially those within the states. The delegates feared also a plebiscitary chief on the national scene or a widespread populistic democracy. Against these dangers, they devised a set of "republican remedies" to apply to the federal gov-ernment itself. Their "republican remedies" had another purpose: to complete and perfect the representative republic itself.

The representative devices in the Constitution serve both to temper political will and to supplement and complete it by pro-viding representation for interests that might otherwise remain unheard. Representation in the Constitution was the subject of sectional and factional compromise. These compromises had also (and were understood to have) a broad tendency to supplement and expand political representation. In sum, the representative arrangements in the Constitution, whatever other purposes they had, were also designed to offset the defects of political represen-tation that arose from an inadequately organized politics.

Sinister Accumulations of Power

Today, we are apt to think of checks and balances, separation of powers, and indirect representation as devices to restrain the "tyranny of the majority," and to thwart popular government. In part they have that effect. But in the eighteenth century, they were good republican and democratic devices and, in fact, applied con-sistently and rigorously by radical republicans in the states. When commending such devices in the Convention, the delegates some-times spoke of the danger of majorities or omnipotent legislatures. A more central concern was cabal and faction: the threats of silent and sinister accumulations of power and of the disruption of the polity by minority interests. The delegates were trying to generate a national will, not defeat it. A central danger, as they saw it, was that such a will would not be representative, that it would be a will proclaiming itself the representative of the whole but masking designs for power, pelf, and preferment. Separation of powers, checks and balances, and representative formulae would work to counteract the natural tendencies of politics built on a primitive economic and social base. Such devices were also vital for nourishing the government itself: to secure confidence in it; to win the support of disinterested patriots; and to afford a security against fecund evils.

A democrat might say that the delegates took too low a view of politics. Perhaps they did. But that judgment misses one of the unique and original contributions of the Founding Fathers. They contrived an alternate and supplementary system of institutions to remedy the deficiencies of their own political society. The delegates' constitutional methods of fragmentation, of withdrawal and delegation, and of nourishing a patriot elite are directed to this object. They wished to stimulate loyalty to the principles of republican government. They wanted also to generate power in the whole system. They sought to achieve both these ends by limiting politics—that is, politics in the ordinary sense of the word. But in constraining and narrowing the method of politics, they supplemented the Constitution, providing for alternate methods, other modes for the resolution of conflict, and for stimulating patriotic energies.

Eighteenth-century philosophers often spoke of a social contract and of a political contract or contract of government. These terms are useful in the present context. The task for the delegates was to build a nationwide political contract upon an untried and possibly inadequate foundation. For this purpose, they required more than a simple principal-agent model of government. Neither the existing society nor contemporary political institutions could sustain a republican government based upon a direct connection between political will and government response. Supporting the political contract required artful measures. Consequently, the delegates contrived methods to strengthen particular political institutions by formal constitutional provisions and to sublimate intense political passions by utilizing the forces of social and economic evolution. American politics was "judicialized." Many issues that involved property, citizenship, and the development of the nation were reserved from the direct or speedy expression of popular will. Even ordinary political decision was closely associated with the politics of federalism and an intricate constitutional system of representation and separation of powers. According to one view of democracy, the delegates dethroned the people and set up an antidemocratic scheme of government. But "politics" in the narrow usage of that term is a small part of the whole of the life of man, and even a small part of what most understand democracy to be. Whether the delegates' conception of the right relation between citizens, the society, and the state, between the social contract and the contract of government, was an ungenerous one or even an antipopular one, remains to be discussed in later chapters. Certainly we can say, however, that their conception was statesmanlike.

To Launch a Nation

The intention of the delegates probably cannot be finally known. But if we establish a purpose that included a wider intention and motive than that imputed by Beard . . . we lay a foundation for the ensuing discussion. Without alleging proof, it would be useful to state what seems the most plausible interpretation of the delegates' intentions.

In the context of their society and their experience with the colonial and revolutionary governments, the delegates' activities in behalf of the new government seem to have been directed primarily at a simple, coherent set of *political* objectives. They seem to have been aiming at (1) withdrawing particular objects of contention from local majorities; (2) attempting to secure a common interest; (3) securing the support for the "representative republic" of a stratum of "wise and virtuous" leaders who would put republican principles above personal and factional interest; and (4) devising a scheme of representation and checks and balances that would complete that government and prevent it in turn from developing cumulative tendencies toward an extreme.

The delegates, in Convention and out of it, appear to have been doing what people have generally thought they were. They protected property, but especially in order to remove sources of discord, foster economic growth, and develop interest in the government. They destroyed the dependence of the government upon the states, but more in the interests of a national citizenship than fear of democracy. Similarly, they added to central government the "salutary checks" of republican government as much to complete a representative will as to restrain it. In Convention and out of it they did not act as if they were trying to execute a *coup* for their faction, defend property, or silence democrats in the states. They were men engaged in a task intellectually and practically of enormous difficulty: to conceive a successful constitution and launch a nation. That task required great initiative and sound principles of strategy and philosophy.

The difficulty of the task answers at least partly the charge of usurpation. Without any doubt the delegates violated their mandate. They also appealed from the Congress and the states to the ratifying conventions. While their deeds lacked constituted political legitimacy, that same defect also puts a different face upon their actions. The Convention was not a government. The delegates could at most hope to persuade the active electorate, assuming that elections to the conventions would be held. Against their cause they had two of the most powerful of political influences: inertia and fear of the unknown. Under the circumstances, the charge of usurpation does not seem a grave one.

Beard . . . reminds us that the Founding Fathers lived long ago and that they made a Constitution to serve, initially, a society of a few million farmers. There is no security that their philosophy will continue to serve us, especially at times when new popular creeds are struggling for recognition. To their credit, however, the Founding Fathers did not finally settle the issue between republican government and responsiveness to popular creeds or democratic majorities. Instead, they initiated a dialogue between the people as ultimate sovereign and the people as *populus*, as trustee for the nation.

"If the members of the Convention . . . expected to derive benefits from the establishment of the new system, so also did most of the people of the country."

The Founders Wrote the Constitution to Protect the Property and Rights of All Americans

Robert E. Brown

Among the leading constitutional scholars who have disagreed with Charles Beard's thesis about the economic motives of the founders is Robert E. Brown, who wrote an entire volume (*Charles Beard and the Constitution*) intended to refute that thesis. According to Brown, Beard's argument is inconsistent because it does not address the issue of how average Americans of the 1780s viewed property. "Since most of the people were middle-class and had private property," says Brown, "practically everybody was interested in the protection of property," and

Robert E. Brown, *Charles Beard and the Constitution*. Princeton, NJ: Princeton University Press, 1956. Copyright © 1956 by Princeton University Press. Reproduced by permission.

"many people believed that the Constitution did not go far enough to protect property." Also, Brown contends, Beard often quoted the Founding Fathers out of context or left out quotes that did not support his agenda.

If historical method means the gathering of data from primary sources, the critical evaluation of the evidence thus gathered, and the drawing of conclusions consistent with this evidence, then we must conclude that Beard has done great violation to such method in this book. He admitted that the evidence had not been collected which, given the proper use of historical method, should have precluded the writing of the book. Yet he nevertheless proceeded on the assumption that a valid interpretation could be built on secondary writings whose authors had likewise failed to collect the evidence. If we accept Beard's own maxim, "no evidence, no history," and his own admission that the data had never been collected, the answer to whether he used historical method properly is self-evident.

Neither was Beard critical of the evidence which he did use. He was accused in 1913, and one might still suspect him, of using only that evidence which appeared to support his thesis. The amount of realty in the country compared with the personalty, the vote in New York, and the omission of the part of *The Federalist* No. 10 which did not fit his thesis are only a few examples of the uncritical use of evidence to be found in the book. Sometimes he accepted secondary accounts at face value without checking them with the sources; at other times he allowed unfounded rumors and traditions to color his work.

Finally, the conclusions which he drew were not justified even by the kind of evidence which he used. If we accepted his evidence strictly at face value, it would still not add up to the fact that the Constitution was put over undemocratically in an undemocratic society by personalty. The citing of property qualifications does not prove that a mass of men were disfranchised. And if we accept his figures on property holdings, either we do not know what most of the delegates had in realty and personalty, or we know that realty outnumbered personalty three to one (eighteen to six).

Simply showing that a man held public securities is not sufficient to prove that he acted only in terms of his public securities. If we ignore Beard's own generalizations and accept only his evidence, we would have to conclude that most of the property in the country in 1787 was real estate, that real property was widely distributed in rural areas, which included most of the country, and that even the men who were directly concerned with the Constitution, and especially Washington, were large holders of realty.

No "Propertyless Masses"

Perhaps we can never be completely objective in history, but certainly we can be more objective than Beard was in this book. Naturally the historian must always be aware of the biases, the subjectivity, the pitfalls that confront him, but this does not mean that he should not make an effort to overcome these obstacles. Whether Beard had his thesis before he had his evidence, as some have said, is a question that each reader must answer for himself. Certain it is that the evidence does not justify the thesis.

So instead of the Beard interpretation that the Constitution was put over undemocratically in an undemocratic society by personal property, the following fourteen paragraphs are offered as a possible interpretation of the Constitution and as suggestions for future research on that document.

1. The movement for the Constitution was originated and carried through by men who had long been important in both economic and political affairs in their respective states. Some of them owned personalty, more of them owned realty, and if their property was adversely affected by conditions under the Articles of Confederation, so also was the property of the bulk of the people in the country, middle-class farmers as well as town artisans.

2. The movement for the Constitution, like most important movements, was undoubtedly started by a small group of men. They were probably interested personally in the outcome of their labors, but the benefits which they expected were not confined to personal property or, for that matter, strictly to things economic. And if their own interests would be enhanced by a new government, similar interests of other men, whether agricultural or commercial, would also be enhanced.

3. Naturally there was no popular vote on the calling of the convention which drafted the Constitution. Election of delegates by state legislatures was the constitutional method under the Articles of Confederation, and had been the method long established in this country. Delegates to the Albany Congress, the Stamp Act Congress, the First Continental Congress, the Second Continental Congress, and subsequent congresses under the Articles were all elected by state legislatures, not by the people. Even the Articles of Confederation had been sanctioned by state legislatures, not by popular vote. This is not to say that the Constitutional Convention should not have been elected directly by the people, but only that such a procedure would have been unusual at the time. Some of the opponents of the Constitution later stressed, without avail, the fact that the Convention had not been directly elected. But at the time the Convention met, the people in general seemed to be about as much concerned over the fact that they had not elected the delegates as the people of this country are now concerned over the fact that they do not elect our delegates to the United Nations.

4. Present evidence seems to indicate that there were no "propertyless masses" who were excluded from the suffrage at the time. Most men were middle-class farmers who owned realty and were qualified voters, and, as the men in the Convention said, mechanics had always voted in the cities. Until credible evidence proves otherwise, we can assume that state legislatures were fairly representative at the time. We cannot condone the fact that a few men were probably disfranchised by prevailing property qualifications, but it makes a great deal of difference to an interpretation of the Constitution whether the disfranchised comprised ninety-five per cent of the adult men or only five per cent. Figures which give percentages of voters in terms of the entire population are misleading, since less than twenty per cent of the people were adult men. And finally, the voting qualifications favored realty, not personalty.

Everybody Was Interested in Property

5. If the members of the Convention were directly interested in the outcome of their work and expected to derive benefits from

the establishment of the new system, so also did most of the people of the country. We have many statements to the effect that the people in general expected substantial benefits from the labors of the Convention.

6. The Constitution was not just an economic document, although economic factors were undoubtedly important. Since most of the people were middle-class and had private property, practically everybody was interested in the protection of property. A constitution which did not protect property would have been rejected without any question, for the American people had fought the Revolution for the preservation of life, liberty, and property. Many people believed that the Constitution did not go far enough to protect property, and they wrote these views into the amendments to the Constitution. But property was not the only concern of those who wrote and ratified the Constitution, and we would be doing a grave injustice to the political sagacity of the Founding Fathers if we assumed that property or personal gain was their only motive.

7. Naturally the delegates recognized that the protection of property was important under government, but they also recognized that personal rights were equally important. In fact, persons and property were usually bracketed together as the chief objects of government protection.

8. If three-fourths of the adult males failed to vote on the election of delegates to ratifying conventions, this fact signified indifference, not disfranchisement. We must not confuse those who could *not* vote with those who *could* vote but failed to exercise their right. Many men at the time bewailed the fact that only a small portion of the voters ever exercised their prerogative. But this in itself should stand as evidence that the conflict over the Constitution was not very bitter, for if these people had felt strongly one way or the other, more of them would have voted.

Even if we deny the evidence which I have presented and insist that American society was undemocratic in 1787, we must still accept the fact that the men who wrote the Constitution believed that they were writing it for a democratic society. They did not hide behind an iron curtain of secrecy and devise the kind of conservative government that they wanted without regard to the views and interests of "the people." More than anything else, they were aware that "the people" would have to ratify what they proposed, and that therefore any government which would be acceptable to the people must of necessity incorporate much of what was customary at the time. The men at Philadelphia were practical politicians, not political theorists. They recognized the multitude of different ideas and interests that had to be reconciled and compromised before a constitution would be acceptable. They were far too practical, and represented far too many clashing interests themselves, to fashion a government weighted in favor of personalty or to believe that the people would adopt such a government.

9. If the Constitution was ratified by a vote of only one-sixth of the adult men, that again demonstrates indifference and not disfranchisement. Of the one-fourth of the adult males who voted, nearly two-thirds favored the Constitution. Present evidence does not permit us to say what the popular vote was except as it was measured by the votes of the ratifying conventions.

10. Until we know what the popular vote was, we cannot say that it is questionable whether a majority of the voters in several states favored the Constitution. Too many delegates were sent uninstructed. Neither can we count the towns which did not send delegates on the side of those opposed to the Constitution. Both items would signify indifference rather than sharp conflict over ratification.

The People Could Have Rejected the Constitution

11. The ratifying conventions were elected for the specific purpose of adopting or rejecting the Constitution. The people in general had anywhere from several weeks to several months to decide the question. If they did not like the new government, or if they did not know whether they liked it, they could have voted *no* and there would have been no Constitution. Naturally the leaders in the ratifying conventions represented the same interests as the members of the Constitutional Convention—mainly realty and some personalty. But they also represented their constituents in these same interests, especially realty.

12. If the conflict over ratification had been between substan-

tial personalty interests on the one hand and small farmers and
debtors on the other, there would not have been a constitution.
The small farmers comprised such an overwhelming percentage
of the voters that they could have rejected the new government
without any trouble. Farmers and debtors are not synonymous
terms and should not be confused as such. A town-by-town or
county-by-county record of the vote would show clearly how the
farmers voted.

13. The Constitution was created about as much by the whole
people as any government could be which embraced a large area
and depended on representation rather than on direct participation. It was also created in part by the states, for as the *Records*
show, there was strong state sentiment at the time which had to
be appeased by compromise. And it was created by compromising a whole host of interests throughout the country, without
which compromises it could never have been adopted.

14. If the intellectual historians are correct, we cannot explain
the Constitution without considering the psychological factors
also. Men are motivated by what they believe as well as by what
they have. Sometimes their actions can be explained on the basis
of what they hope to have or hope that their children will have.
Madison understood this fact when he said that the universal hope
of acquiring property tended to dispose people to look favorably
upon property. It is even possible that some men support a given
economic system when they themselves have nothing to gain by
it. So we would want to know what the people in 1787 thought of
their class status. Did workers and small farmers believe that they
were lower-class, or did they, as many workers do now, consider
themselves middle-class? Were the common people trying to
eliminate the Washingtons, Adamses, Hamiltons, and Pinckneys,
or were they trying to join them?

Support for Beard "An Act of Faith"?

As did Beard's fourteen conclusions, these fourteen suggestions
really add up to two major propositions: the Constitution was
adopted in a society which was fundamentally democratic, not
undemocratic; and it was adopted by a people who were primarily middle-class property owners, especially farmers who owned

realty, not just by the owners of personalty. At present these points seem to be justified by the evidence, but if better evidence in the future disproves or modifies them, we must accept that evidence and change our interpretation accordingly.

After this critical analysis, we should at least not begin future research on this period of American history with the illusion that the Beard thesis of the Constitution is valid. If historians insist on accepting the Beard thesis in spite of this analysis, however, they must do so with the full knowledge that their acceptance is founded on "an act of faith," not an analysis of historical method, and that they are indulging in a "noble dream," not history.

For Further Discussion

Chapter 1
1. Compare and contrast the arguments for and against keeping the Articles of Confederation, as voiced by Melancton Smith and Benjamin Rush. What is Rush's telling point about British history that he feels Americans can learn from?
2. After reading Jackson Turner Main's essay about Anti-Federalists' fears of military dictatorship, do you feel that he has made a strong case? Why or why not? In your opinion, would such concerns about military control of the government be justified today? Why or why not?

Chapter 2
1. Where did James Madison and the other framers get their ideas for a system of checks and balances? Briefly describe these safeguards, citing the three branches of government.
2. Explain the conditions under which checks and balances would not be needed, as argued by Samuel Bryan. What governmental model did Bryan cite and how was it structured?
3. Why, according to Patrick Henry, did the Constitution need a bill of rights? Cite some of the depredations he warned might occur if no such bill was adopted.

Chapter 3
1. People today take for granted the idea that slavery is morally wrong and should not be allowed to exist. But the founders grew up in a society in which the institution of slavery was taken more or less for granted, especially in the American South, where much of the economy was based on slave labor. After reading the essays by James Wilson and the Pennsylvania Society for the Abolition of Slavery, describe the arguments' points for and against banning the slave trade at the time.
2. Given the economic and social traditions and conditions of the late 1700s, should American slave owners of that era, including some of the Constitution's framers, be forgiven for their

failure to ban slavery in the document? Or should they be criticized for not having the courage of their convictions? Why?
Use points made in the essays by Herbert J. Storing and Thurgood Marshall.

Chapter 4

1. The noted historian Clinton Rossiter argues that the success of
   the Constitution should be attributed mostly to the political
   genius of the founders. If you agree with his thesis, cite four of
   the many examples he gives of major and insightful contributions made by various framers. If, on the other hand, you agree
   more with Alfred F. Young's argument—that the founders had
   no choice but to appease the demands of the people—cite four
   points Young makes to support his view.
2. Summarize Charles A. Beard's controversial proposition about
   the motives of the Constitution's framers. List each of the five
   points he cites from James Madison's discussion of the importance of property rights. Do you agree or disagree with Madison?
   Why or why not? In your opinion, does Beard make a strong case
   for the selfish interests of the founders? Why or why not?
3. Contrast the motives David G. Smith suggests for the framers
   with those suggested by Beard.
4. Cite four of the reasons that Robert E. Brown contends make
   Beard's thesis inconsistent or otherwise faulty. Is Brown's
   point—that the people could have rejected the Constitution
   during the ratification period but did not do so—convincing?
   Why or why not?

✵ Chronology

November 15, 1777

The Continental Congress votes to adopt the Articles of Confederation, which to become official must be ratified by the thirteen states.

March 1, 1781

Maryland becomes the last of the thirteen states to ratify and sign the Articles of Confederation.

November 23, 1786

Virginia is the first state to authorize sending delegates to Philadelphia to attend a convention that will consider revising the articles.

February 21, 1787

The Continental Congress officially authorizes the Philadelphia Constitutional Convention.

May 25, 1787

The delegates from the states meet in Philadelphia and elect George Washington as president of the convention. The delegates decide that matters will be decided by majority vote and that each state will have one vote. (In the days that follow, the consensus becomes that the articles should be scrapped and a new constitution adopted.)

June 19, 1787

The delegates debate the issue of whether the states should have equal or proportional representation in the national legislature.

July 13, 1787

As the convention continues in Philadelphia, the Continental Congress, meeting in New York, votes to adopt the Northwest Ordinance. This plan provides for the future creation of states in the Ohio Valley and guarantees freedom of worship, trial by jury, and public education in that region. It also prohibits slavery in the same area.

July 16, 1787

The delegates in Philadelphia reach a compromise and divide the new national legislature into two houses—the House of Representatives, with proportional representation, and the Senate, with equal state representation.

August 6–September 10, 1787

The delegates grant Congress the right to regulate foreign trade and interstate commerce, as well as allow the slave trade to remain in effect for at least twenty more years. They also set up a system in which elections will take place every four years for president, every six years for senators, and every two years for members of the House of Representatives.

September 12, 1787

A completed rough draft of the Constitution (written mainly by Gouveneur Morris of New York) is submitted to the convention. Virginia's George Mason proposes adding a bill of rights to the document. The motion is defeated.

September 15, 1787

A delegate proposes that a second convention be held to add amendments to the Constitution. This motion is defeated and the convention approves the document.

September 17, 1787

Thirty-nine of the forty-two delegates sign the Constitution and the convention adjourns.

September 20–28, 1787

The Continental Congress receives the signed copy of the Constitution and, after some debate, decides to submit the document to a series of state ratifying conventions. A minimum of nine states must ratify it before it can take effect.

October 27, 1787

The first of eighty-five essays, later collected as the *Federalist Papers*, appears in a New York newspaper. Written by James Madison, Alexander Hamilton, and John Jay, these writings support the provisions of the Constitution and respond to criticisms of the document.

December 7, 1787
Delaware becomes the first state to ratify the Constitution.

December 12, 1787
Pennsylvania ratifies the Constitution.

January 9, 1788
Connecticut becomes the fifth state to ratify.

March 1788
Rhode Island lawmakers call for the people to vote on the Constitution. After local Federalists boycott the election, the state rejects the Constitution.

June 21, 1788
As New Hampshire becomes the ninth state to ratify the Constitution, the document goes into effect.

June 25, 1788
The Virginia ratifying convention proposes adding a bill of rights to the Constitution.

July 26, 1788
New York ratifies the Constitution. North Carolina and Rhode Island remain the only holdouts.

November 21, 1789
North Carolina ratifies.

May 29, 1790
Rhode Island ratifies.

January 10, 1791
The newly formed state of Vermont, the fourteenth in the Union, ratifies the Constitution.

December 15, 1791
The Bill of Rights—comprised of the first ten amendments to the Constitution—is ratified.

For Further Research

Books

John K. Alexander, *The Selling of the Constitutional Convention.* Madison, WI: Madison House, 1990.

Thornton Anderson, *Creating the Constitution.* University Park: Pennsylvania State University Press, 1993.

Fred Barbash, *The Founding: A Dramatic Account of the Writing of the Constitution.* New York: Simon and Schuster, 1987.

Charles A. Beard, *An Economic Interpretation of the Constitution.* New York: Macmillan, 1913. Reprint, New York: Free Press, 1986.

Richard B. Bernstein, *Amending America.* New York: Times Books, 1993.

Catherine D. Bowers, *Miracle at Philadelphia: The Story of the Constitutional Convention, May to September 1787.* Boston: Little, Brown, 1966.

Julian P. Boyd, ed., *The Papers of Thomas Jefferson.* 60 vols. (projected). Princeton, NJ: Princeton University Press, 1950– .

Robert E. Brown, *Charles Beard and the Constitution.* New York: W.W. Norton, 1956.

Jonathan Elliot, ed., *The Debates in the Several State Conventions on the Adoption of the Federal Constitution, etc., etc.* New York: Burt Franklin, 1888.

Joseph J. Ellis, *The Founding Brothers: The Revolutionary Generation.* New York: Knopf, 2000.

Paul L. Ford, ed., *Pamphlets on the Constitution of the United States, Published During Its Discussion by the People, 1787–1788.* Brooklyn, NY: Historical Printing Club, 1888.

Thurston Greene, *The Language of the Constitution.* New York: Greenwood, 1991.

Robert H. Horwitz, ed., *The Moral Foundations of the American Republic.* Charlottesville: University Press of Virginia, 1986.

Galliard Hunt, ed., *The Writings of James Madison, 1783–1787.* 9 vols. New York: G.P. Putnam's Sons, 1901.

Merrill Jensen, *The Making of the American Constitution.* New York: Van Nostrand, 1964.

Alfred H. Kelly et al., *The American Constitution, Its Origins and Development.* New York: Norton, 1991.

Adrienne Koch and William Peden, eds., *The Life and Selected Writings of Thomas Jefferson.* New York: Random House, 1944.

Thomas Lloyd, ed., *Debates of the Convention of the State of Pennsylvania on the Constitution Proposed for the United States.* Philadelphia, 1788.

Milton Lomask, *The Spirit of 1787: The Making of Our Constitution.* New York: Ballantine, 1980.

Jackson Turner Main, *The Antifederalists: The Critics of the Constitution, 1781–1788.* Chapel Hill: University of North Carolina Press, 1961.

Samuel Eliot Morison, *The Oxford History of the American People.* New York: Oxford University Press, 1965.

Hezekiah Niles, ed., *Principles and Acts of the Revolution in America.* Baltimore: W.O. Niles, 1822.

J.R. Pole, ed., *The American Constitution, For and Against: The Federalist and Anti-Federalist Papers.* New York: Hill and Wang, 1987.

Jack N. Rakove, *Original Meanings: Politics and Ideas in the Making of the Constitution.* New York: Vintage, 1996.

David Robertson, ed., *Debates and Other Proceedings of the Convention of Virginia.* Richmond, VA: Inquirer, 1805.

Clinton Rossiter, *1787: The Grand Convention*. New York: W.W. Norton, 1966.

Robert A. Rutland, *James Madison: Founding Father*. New York: Macmillan, 1987.

———, ed., *The Papers of George Mason, 1725–1792*. Chapel Hill: University of North Carolina Press, 1970.

Bernard Schwartz, *The Reins of Power: A Constitutional History of the United States*. New York: Hill and Wang, 1963.

David G. Smith, *The Convention and the Constitution: The Political Ideas of the Founding Fathers*. New York: St. Martin's Press, 1965.

Herbert J. Storing, *What the Anti-Federalists Were For*. Chicago: University of Chicago Press, 1981.

Helen E. Veit et al., eds., *Creating the Bill of Rights: The Documentary Record from the First Federal Congress*. Baltimore: Johns Hopkins University Press, 1991.

Periodicals

Samuel Bryan, "To the Freemen of Pennsylvania, from Centinel," *Independent Gazetteer*, October 5, 1787.

E.L. Doctorow, "A Citizen Reads the Constitution," *Nation*, February 21, 1987.

John Greenwald, "A Gift to All Nations," *Time*, July 6, 1987.

Alexander Hamilton, "Open Letter to the People of the State of New York, from Publius," *Independent Journal*, May 1788.

Bruce G. Kauffmann, "James Madison: Godfather of the Constitution," *Early America Review*, Summer 1997.

James Madison, "Open Letter to the People of the State of New York, from Publius," *Independent Journal*, February 1788.

Alfred F. Young, "The Framers of the Constitution and the 'Genius' of the People," *Radical History Review*, Fall 1988.

Internet Sources

Charles Beard, essay from *Framing the Constitution*, School of Co-operative Individualism. www.cooperativeindividualism.org/beard_constitution.html.

Charters of Freedom, "Constitution of the United States," National Archives. www.archives.gov/national_archives_experience/constitution.html.

Library of Congress, "Documents from the Continental Congress and Constitutional Convention, 1774–1789." http://lcweb2.loc.gov/ammem/bdsd/bdsdhome.html.

———, "The U.S. Constitution." www.usconstitution.net/const.html.

U.S. Constitution Online, "Articles of the Confederation." www.usconstitution.net/articles.html.

✵ Index

✵ About the Editor

Historian and award-winning author Don Nardo has written or edited many books for young people about American history, including *The Bill of Rights, The War of 1812, The Mexican-American War, The Great Depression, Pearl Harbor*, and biographies of Thomas Jefferson, Andrew Johnson, and Franklin D. Roosevelt. Mr. Nardo lives with his wife, Christine, in Massachusetts.